YOUR I

FIFTEEN PAGES

YOUR FIRST FIFTEEN PAGES

An agent's guide to writing a novel that agents will champion, editors will publish and readers will buy!

Sandra O'Donnell, Ph.D.

RO PUBLISHING

RO Publishing
RO Literary, LLC
La Jolla, CA 92037
www.roliterary.com
www.roliterary/ropublishling.com

ISBN: 978-1732298200 (trade paperback)

10 9 8 7 6 5 4 3 2 1

"Read, read, read. Read everything—trash, classics, good and bad; see how they do it. When a carpenter learns his trade, he does so by observing.

Read! You'll absorb it.

William Faulkner

Contents

Introduction

"It's none of their business that you have to learn to write. Let them think you were born that way."

—*Ernest Hemingway*

What is the difference between a writer who never finds an agent or sells her manuscript to a publisher and an author who becomes a best seller? *The first fifteen pages.* If you have been sending out queries and wonder why your manuscript hasn't grabbed the interest of an agent, the answer might be in the first fifteen pages you submitted. Why? Because quite simply, most submissions are missing one or more of the crucial elements needed for a writer to go from unrepresented, to signed by an agent, to a book contract, to a *major* book contract.

The job, the explicit goal, of those critical first fifteen pages, is to hook agents, editors, and ultimately readers. Those first pages need to grab us if not by the collar, at least by the sleeve and say, "I've got you. Keep reading." If your first fifteen pages don't do that, your manuscript won't make it past an agent's slush pile, and your book will never land in the hands of a reader or brighten the screen of their Kindles.

As a literary agent, I've read thousands of queries and thousands of beginning pages. I've learned what makes a submission story sing, and what sends me back to the author's query to find an email so I can ask for more. And, I've learned what causes me, more often than not, to push *Send* on a "passed with love" email.

I loathe having to send those "thanks but no thanks" responses to a writer's work. I don't know any agent who looks forward to the opportunity to gleefully kill the dreams of someone who has spent years toiling away on a book.

Being an agent requires having an endless fountain of hope. Every day, I open queries just knowing that today will be the day I discover the next Liane Moriarty, JK Rowling, or Erik Larson. Every time we read a query, we do it with renewed faith that this query just might be the one.

Sadly, in the last two years, our agency has requested fewer than 50 full manuscripts from all the submissions we've read. Fewer than 50! Why? Because by page fifteen of most submissions, the hope and excitement we had on page one are dashed.

Fifteen pages may seem an unfairly short or arbitrary number of pages to determine if the writing or the story is worth pursuing. But honestly, by reading the first fifteen pages of a manuscript, I know what I need to know, which is:

- If the writing is fresh, beautifully wrought, moving, or exceptional.

- What drove the story into being – the inciting incident.

- Who the main characters are and what makes them interesting and distinct.

- When and where the story is set – the time frame, place, or historical period.

- The genre – is the story a romance set in Tuscany, a WWII revisionist history, a coming of age LGBTQ, a YA dystopian set in the past, or commercial fiction about life after death?

- If the point of view feels right for the story.

- If the writer is the only person who has read the manuscript. (A dead give away is a manuscript riddled with grammatical errors with big holes in the story.)

And, most importantly, we know if it is a story we are passionate about or at least excited enough about after fifteen pages to ask for the full manuscript. We know if we are hooked, if you have indeed grabbed us if not by the collar, at least the sleeve, and said, "I've got you. Ask for more so you can see what happens next."

The job of the writer is *not* to merely string words together on a page but to place those words so artfully, so strategically that we, the reader, keep asking for more by turning the page. Your writing needs to propel us to the next scene and urge us to read just one more chapter even when we have work to do, kids to pick up, deadlines to finish, and dinners to prepare. That is the hallmark of excellent writing – *a book that is impossible to put down.*

Do we really need another book on writing? Yes! While there are already numerous books on writing on the market, few point out how crucial it is to engage the reader with the essential elements of your story in the first pages of your novel. The few that do, books such as *The First Five Pages* by Noah Lukeman, are unnecessarily dense and set the unrealistic objective for writers to establish their story in the first five pages. Try as I might, I came up short for examples of books that provided readers with enough of the story or a reason to keep reading after page five. The flipside of the too short dilemma is *The First Fifty Pages* by Jeff Gerke. Unfortunately, most writers find that if they haven't nailed their story down much earlier, by the time they reach page fifty, they are wandering in the weeds trying to get their characters and story back on track.

Fifteen pages are the Goldilocks choice for storytelling. Not too short, not too long, but just the right amount of time for us to become engaged in your story. If we aren't into your story by page fifteen, our attention wanders, and after that, it is very difficult to get the reader back. I can hear many of you groaning, "My story is special. I need more time to develop my characters to give a backstory to build tension to pile on all the things I learned in writing classes!" Actually, you don't. All you need to introduce the essential elements – the who, what, where, when, and most importantly the why of your story – are the first fifteen pages. In this book, I back up my reasons for concentrating on the first fifteen pages by sharing examples from the bestselling novels in a variety of genres.

Need more proof? After reading the first two chapters of this book Kamara, Sarah, and Mandy, members of a co-writing group, went to a xiv | YOUR FIRST FIFTEEN PAGES

bookstore and spent "a couple of hours pulling books off the shelves and reading the first fifteen pages." Sarah was skeptical, "I didn't think what I'd read would hold up, but it did! Book after book, fifteen pages after fifteen pages, we kept seeing that you were right. The inciting incident, the characters, the setting, and the actions were all clearly defined in those first fifteen pages of our favorite books. We were hooked!"

You don't have to take my word for it. Read the first two chapters of this book and then pick up your favorite book in your favorite genre. Read the first fifteen pages. See for yourself what drew you to the book and why you kept reading.

In *Your First Fifteen Pages*, I unpack the mystery of what it takes to capture and hold the interest of agents, editors, and ultimately readers. I explain why agents move on to the next query, and the next, passing on manuscripts that we feel won't live up to a reader's expectations. And most importantly for you the writer, I show you how to perfect your first fifteen pages, and in doing so, help you fix many of the problems with the remainder of your novel or keep obstacles at bay if you're just getting started.

I want to help you get past the slush pile and open the door for "the big ask" every writer dreams of – a request for a full manuscript read, an offer of representation and ultimately a book contract. While I can't guarantee your book will be signed or become a best seller, I can give you a solid foundation for the story you dream of telling, which will put you far ahead of those also competing for the attention of agents and editors.

This book is for beginning writers AND for those who have a pile of thanks but no thanks rejections sitting in their inbox. It is for the novice writer with an inkling of a book idea AND for those who've heard crickets from all the queries they've sent out. It is for those who dream of being on a bestseller list or winning a major book award, AND for those who want to write the best book possible and see where it takes them.

I am in the business of books because I love great stories, and I love helping the people who write them. I do what I do because I want to discover your work, help your book grow, and see you on a bestseller list someday.

Join me and let's get started on your first fifteen pages!

Chapter 1: Elements of Story

If you make the right decision about structure, many other things become absolutely clear. On some level, the rest is easy.

—*Nora Ephron*

Have you ever stopped to think about what makes a great story great? What keeps a reader reading past the first chapter or two? Of course, you have . . . Haven't you?

Most writers think they know what makes a story work. Academically trained writers, those with MFAs, who took creative writing classes in college or grad school and studied character, dialogue, pacing, setting, and developed a myriad of craft tools believe they have the skills to write a prize-winning novel. The flipside of the MFA trained writer is someone who began her writing career after reading a mediocre novel and thinking, "I bet I can write better than that!" She bought a few books on writing, or she didn't, and she dove into her YA, historical fiction, or thriller, learning as she went.

Surprisingly, neither has an edge when it comes to our query list. We pass on submissions by MFA, Pushcart Prize-winning writers as often, if not more often, than those submitted by untrained writers with a passion for storytelling.

Why? Because their submissions–the first fifteen pages of their manuscripts–are missing some or most of the basic elements of storytelling. Both the MFA trained writer and the novice, more often than not, fail to define for the reader the who, what, where, when, or why of their story in those crucial early pages. When one or more of those elements are nebulous or are entirely missing from the first fifteen pages, we pass.

Why are these elements essential? Let's look at a basic story. A story we might tell a friend or a co-worker.

"Oh my god! You won't believe what happened to me on the way to work today. I was getting on the train and that guy, the really menacing looking guy I told you about, the one . . . "

Laura jumps in, "You mean the one who always wears the 1970s Adidas tracksuit and tennis shoes? The guy who had that pink and purple paisley kid's backpack with him the other day?"

"Yes, that guy. Well, today I was watching him, wondering for the fiftieth time where he goes every day in his tracksuit with that odd backpack when I got a text telling me not to come in until 11:00 because they are fumigating the office and of course Tali forget to tell us all yesterday. So, I decided what the hell, I'm going to stay on the train and see what he does."

"Are you crazy? He could be a murderer! Why did you do that?"

"I don't know. Something just told me not to get off. So I pretended to be so engrossed in the book I was reading, I didn't hear my stop called."

"What happened?"

Well, I kept waiting and waiting. A ton of frickin' stops went by. When we crossed the river, I thought, shit, he's never getting off this stupid train what a waste of time. Finally, when we got to Prospect Park, he picked up the backpack and got off."

"And? Did you follow him?"

"No by that time, I was running late for work. But as I was watching him walk down the platform, this other guy sitting on a bench at the far end of the stop got up and started following him. The whole thing is so weird. I'm going to take tomorrow off and follow him again."

"I'm going with you!"

All the elements needed for a good story are there.

WHO	Two friends, a weird guy on a train, and a mysterious person at the train stop.
WHAT	Discussing the actions of an odd man one of the friends has been observing for some time.
WHERE	On a train.
WHEN	Earlier that day as one of the friends was going to work.
WHY	Because the actions of the mysterious guy have been intriguing to one of the characters for a long time, and today she is on the train with time to kill and can follow the mystery man.

Too many submissions we read lack some or most of the essential elements of storytelling. When we read the first fifteen pages of stories and find it is missing fundamental story elements, we ask:

"What is this story about?"

"Who are the main characters?"

"Why should I care about these characters or get involved in this story?"

"Where is this story set?"

"What is the timeframe for this story?"

"What is the point?"

Let's imagine the conversation between the friends again without the essential elements of storytelling in place.

"Oh my god! You won't believe what happened to me on the way to work today. I was on the train when I got a text telling me not to come in until 11 because they are fumigating the office and of course, Tali forget to tell us all yesterday. So, I decided what the hell, I'm going to stay on the train."

"Why would you do that?"

"I don't know something just told me not to get off. So I stayed past my stop pretending to be so engrossed in the book I was reading I didn't hear my stop called."

"So what happened?"

Well, I kept waiting and waiting. A ton of frickin' stops went by.

"And?

"By that time, I was running late for work."

Your friend is wondering why you told them that story. What was so interesting about you riding on a train all morning? Without the intrigue and the decision to follow the mysterious tracksuit wearing guy, without the fact that you've been watching him for weeks, without the backpack, or your overly suspicious nature, this is merely a boring story about riding a train.

Unfortunately, that is true of many of the submissions we receive. The writer began with a captivating premise or character, but once the writing started, the premise or character was left hanging in time and space without any reason for being on the page. Without the details provided by a fully realized *who, what, where, when,* and *why,* we have no idea where the story is headed or why we should keep reading.

Often this is because the writer believes that holding back essential details will keep the reader in suspense. An author I'm working with recently sent me the first third of his novel. The first fifteen pages contained a prologue set long in the past with an unnamed character I assumed would be important later in the story taking obscure actions that were unclear to me as a reader. The prologue was followed by a throwaway courtroom scene that didn't reflect the true nature or character of his protagonist and ultimately had absolutely nothing to do with the story. The inciting incident – the event that triggered the overall story arc – was buried on page 111 of the manuscript. There were characters running around on the page, but without an inciting incident, I had no idea why they were doing what they were doing. Had the writer not already been a client, I would have stopped on page 15 and said, "thanks but no thanks."

The essential elements of storytelling provide readers with signposts that keep us reading and wanting to know more. Without those key signposts, we stop reading because we are wondering where the story is going or if we should bother to keep reading. That is *not* the reaction we want readers to have. The questions we want the reader to ask are those that keep them focused on what happens next.

To get and keep your reader engaged in your story you need to provide necessary signposts for them in the first fifteen pages.

Creating Signposts for Your Reader

While getting your reader to ask what happens next may seem a simple task, it is harder to do than it appears, especially when you only have the first fifteen pages of a manuscript to get them fully engaged. So how do you get us fully invested in your story in the first fifteen pages? By including the basic who, what, where, when, and why signposts that are the hallmarks of a great story.

Here are the signposts that should appear in the first fifteen pages:

WHO	The main characters — the two, three or four main characters that move the story forward in distinct and engaging ways.
WHAT	The actions of the character used to define that character's traits or create tension in the story.
WHERE	The setting — the place where the story occurs.
WHEN	The timeframe or historical period for the story.
WHY	The inciting incident – the reason the story exists.

Let's look at an example of how these signposts work in a book many of us have read.

In *Harry Potter and the Sorcerer's Stone*, JK Rowling uses the first fifteen pages of the story to introduce us to some of the main characters, locate us firmly in place, and provide a clear inciting incident. She also uses "what" to define her characters, create tension, and move the story along. The only element that is nebulous in those first fifteen pages is time. Rowling made strategic use of time in her books. She wanted children to discover her books year after year and not have the story seem stale or dated for future readers. By keeping the timeframe nebulous, she achieves that goal. And there is another genius to her use of time that isn't apparent until you read the second book in the series. She begins each book on Privet Drive, and at the end of each book, Harry must return to his aunt and uncle's house, giving each book, and each encounter with Voldemort, a definitive beginning and ending.

Rowling's introduction of eight major characters in the first chapter of a middle-grade novel is not something I would recommend to novice writers. However, the way she introduces each character using thick, tight descriptions is masterful and provides a study in character – the "who" of a story.

Rowling draws a vivid picture of each character for the reader by linking well-chosen physical attributes to distinguishing traits. Let's look at the first characters we meet, Mr. and Mrs. Dursley. By the end of the second paragraph, we know that the Dursleys are "perfectly normal" and they are not the type of people to "be involved in anything strange or mysterious." We know that Mr. Dursley works for a firm that makes drills and that he is a "big beefy man with hardly any neck" and a "large mustache." We know that Mrs. Dursley is "thin and blonde" and spends her time "craning over garden fences, spying on the neighbors." And we know they have a young son named Dudley who we learn a few pages later has tantrums and throws "his cereal against the wall." Something his parents find charming, rather than disturbing. We have already begun to picture them in our minds. How is that possible with so little description?

Rowling understands that most of us have encountered a Mr. Dursley somewhere along the way. She knows that by giving us a few vital details such as the Dursleys' pride in being normal and Mr. Dursley being "beefy" with "hardly any neck" our minds will fill in the rest and give us a mental picture for that character. The *who* signpost helps us form an image of the character and a relationship between reader and character.

Using character, Rowling also sets us in place. The Dursleys are suburban people, living in a suburban neighborhood where men go to work and mothers stay home and "gossip over fences." With only those few details our minds fill in the rest of the scene – cookie cutter houses, trimmed yards, picket fences.

On page two, we learn that the Dursleys' have a secret and their greatest fear in life is that someone will find out about it. The secret is a "what" signpost. To find out what the secret is, we need to keep reading. We learn that Mrs. Dursley's sister was married to a man named Potter and that the Potters could not be more unlike the Dursleys. The Potters also have a small son, but given how awful the Potters are, how unlike the Dursleys they are, the Dursleys have stayed as far away from the Potters as possible.

On the next page, Rowling tells us that the day begins like any other. The family had breakfast, Mrs. Dursley gossiped, Mr. Dursley picked up his briefcase and headed out to work, and Dudley had a tantrum. Then she shows us how the day rapidly becomes quite unusual by relating what happened to Mr. Dursley throughout the day. On his way to work, Mr. Dursley noticed "peculiar" things, "a cat reading a map" and "a lot of strangely dressed people . . . whispering excitedly." He didn't see the owls "swooping" past his office window "in broad daylight." During the morning he "yelled at five different people" and made "important calls." At lunch, he passed more oddly dressed people, and as he passed them, he heard, "The Potters."

Here is another signpost. By showing us the odd people Mr. Dursley sees during the day and their unusual actions, Rowling is signaling to the reader that something has changed. To learn what, we have to keep reading.

Rowling then tells us that the Dursleys' worst fear, their secret – the Potters – is being discussed in the street. And although this fear jolts

Mr. Dursley, he is determined to act normal and not let on to his wife what he's overheard. But, after hearing a report about the strange behavior of owls throughout the day on the news, he breaks down and asks if Mrs. Dursley has heard from her sister, which causes his wife to become angry. There is something so abhorrent about the Potters, and Mrs. Dursley's sister, that the Dursleys have agreed not to discuss them. We have another *what* signpost – What makes these Potters so awful so horrible that the Dursleys have to keep their relationship to them a secret? To find that out, the reader must keep reading.

As Mr. Dursley is falling asleep, he takes comfort in realizing that even if the Potters were up to something nefarious, "there was no reason for them to come near him and Mrs. Dursley." The page ends with, "How very wrong he was." This statement is a signpost prompting us to keep reading to find out *what* makes him wrong.

While Mr. Dursley is sleeping, a man (a new character), "never seen before on Privet Drive," walks down the street. Rowling begins her description with common traits – tall, thin, and very old, with a silver beard and hair. She then adds layers of very distinct characteristics to give us a clear vision of Albus Dumbledore. His beard and hair were "both long enough to tuck into his belt." He wore "long robes, a purple cloak that swept the ground, high-heeled, buckled boots" and "half-moon spectacles." With that tight description, most of us conjured up an image of who Albus Dumbledore is in our heads. And for most of us, the Dumbledore in our heads looked very much like the Dumbledore portrayed by Richard Harris in the movie.

Next, we meet Professor McGonagall, "a rather severe-looking woman . . . wearing square glasses," an emerald cloak, with her black hair "drawn into a tight bun."

And, we get our first glimmer of Voldemort. And here again, Rowling demonstrates a keen sense of how to build a character arc not just for this book, but one that will carry through all seven books in the series. There is a distinct lack of physical description in the section about Voldemort. And there is a reason for this. In the first few books, Voldemort morphs from a name to a shadow, to a memory, to a parasite, to something less than human. It isn't until the fourth book that Voldemort becomes flesh and bone again.

Rather than describe him physically, Rowling
mystery by only providing his name and the moniko
used by people too frightened to say his name. We lea
is through his actions. He is a murderer who killed
Potter and tried to kill Harry Potter, the Dursleys' nephew
to kill Harry, he disappears because the effort "broke" his p
we have a revealing signpost. We wonder, what kind of power.

Now we know that Harry Potter is an orphan. On page 12, Harry
from being part of the Dursley's biggest secret and worst fear to
orphan who, by page 14, will be left on the Dursleys' doorstep along
with a letter. And here we have a crucial signpost – the why – for the
first book in the series and all the remaining books. Having been
orphaned by Voldemort, Harry must come to live with his only
relatives, the Dursleys, who both fear and despise him even though
they have never met him.

Now we are invested. We want to know what happens next because we
are wondering:

> *What will happen to Harry?*
>
> *Will the Dursleys let him stay?*
>
> *Will they be nice to him or treat him horribly?*
>
> *Who is this Voldemort person?*
>
> *Why are the Dursley so afraid of Harry and his family?*

Notice too that Rowling never uses the words magic, wizard, or spell in
the first few chapters. She alludes to Voldemort's "power" and magic
through the actions of Dumbledore, Professor McGonagall, and
Hagrid. But we, the reader, don't discover Harry is a wizard until Harry
himself makes that discovery. Rowling reveals what she needs to, to
keep us interested and reading but doesn't unveil Harry's real talent or
Hogwarts until later in the book.

Rowling packs all of the essential elements of her story into those
fifteen pages – the who, the what, the where, and the why and alludes
to the when but with a valid reason for keeping it less obvious. Each of
the actions taken by the characters works as a signpost, moving the

story along, revealing information, or helping to develop the story's characters. There are no wasted lines. No detail that isn't directly related to the purpose of the first fifteen pages – orienting the reader to the who, what, where, when and why of the story. Whether you are a fan of the *Harry Potter* series or not, this book is an excellent example of the power of the first fifteen pages.

A Publishing Success Story	Before it found a home at Scholastic and sold millions of copies, numerous agents and publishers rejected *Harry Potter and the Sorcerer's Stone*. Agents and editors passed because the books veered away from many of the standards for middle-grade publishing. The books were considered too long and too complicated for young readers. Thankfully, an editor at Scholastic recognized the brilliance in the books. Readers certainly have, the series has sold more than 500 million copies to date (February 2018). Children and adults all over the world have read and enjoyed Rowling's books.

Had Rowling's first fifteen pages not been as powerful as they are, Harry, Ron, and Hermione might never have graced our library shelves or made it to the big screen. Those first fifteen pages were crucial, especially given how radical the stories seemed for the genre.

Throughout the remainder of this book, we will use successful examples from five different genres to apply the concepts we discuss. And I will throw in a few others from time to time to include other genres.

While some of you might bristle at the use of some of these books, they were picked specifically *because* they were commercially successful. They are also highly engaging, entertaining and offer a satisfying read. Three of the books I've chosen became films. Yes, it is possible for books to be both well written and make money. Why not aim for both?

The books we will be using as exemplars are:

The Firm by John Grisham – *thriller*

The Husband's Secret by Liane Moriarty – *women's fiction*

Harry Potter and the Sorcerer's Stone by J.K. Rowling – *middle grade to young adult*

The Invention of Wings by Sue Monk Kidd – *historical fiction*

The Hunger Games by Suzanne Collins – *young adult, dystopian*

Three of the five books on the list were debut novels. Two are by authors with at least two previous books. They are all easy to find in either your local bookstore or online. I highly recommend you buy a copy of each of these books and read and reread the opening pages as you follow along with the discussion in the remaining chapters.

As you become familiar with the principles we discuss, apply them to your favorite books in your genre. You will see you were drawn to a particular story because it contained all the elements we are discussing here in a way that kept you reading!

We will also be using examples from unpublished manuscripts with the permission of the writers who submitted them to show you what doesn't work and why.

There is no "right" way to use this book. Read it straight through or skip to a chapter that jumps out at you or you feel you need specific help with. While I've tried to put the chapters into an order that makes sense for me, it might make more sense for you to start with setting rather than character because your story is more world driven than character driven. However you use this book, I hope the advice offered is helpful and that it furthers you along on your writing journey.

Your First 15

Not every writer begins with the intention of becoming a novelist or writing a memoir. Many writers are simply compelled to get thoughts and ideas on paper and 20,000 words later, realize they are writing a book. We celebrate writers at all levels. Telling your story is an adventure. For some, the adventure begins with detailed plans, maps, and a cruise director or two leading the way. These writers read books on writing, take classes, write daily, use prompts, and follow writers and writing teachers, honing their craft before even beginning their novel. Others wander along the path, taking in the sites and going wherever their muse leads. Whether you've dedicated years developing your writing chops or this is your first foray into writing, here are a few terms that will help you along the way.

Inciting Incident	In the first fifteen pages, the inciting incident is the event that hooks your reader. For example, in *The Husband's Secret,* the inciting incident is the moment Cecilia finds the envelope addressed to her with the words…"to be opened only"… at the time of her husband's death.
Genre	Think of genre as the way books are shelved in the bookstore. Books are first divided into fiction and nonfiction. Fiction stories describe imaginary people and events. The exception to this rule is historical fiction, which borrows from the lives of real people and events to create fictionalized accounts of the past. Nonfiction books deal with real people, events, and places. After books are divided into fiction and nonfiction, they are further divided into genres. See the table below for a list the fiction genres you might find in a bookstore or browsing on Amazon. Drama—tend to be solemn stories about facing reality head on. Examples: *The Fault is in Our Stars, To Kill a Mockingbird, The Great Gatsby*

Comedy—make fun of the world or an aspect of life. Examples: *The Hitchhiker's Guide to the Galaxy*, *The Commitments*, *Bridget Jones' Diary* (which is also women's fiction).

Literary Fiction —a difficult genre to pull off because everyone is a critic and these books must achieve beautiful writing and tackle something important. Examples: *A Room with a View, Sophie's Choice, All the Light We Cannot See*

Historical Fiction—stories that draw on facts of history or biography to weave a narrative. Examples: *The Orphan Mother, People of the Book*, and *The Invention of Wings*.

Realism—stories that put you in the courtroom or in a specific place and time. Examples: *The Grapes of Wrath, The Jungle*, and *She's Come Undone*

Fantasy—stories of wonder and imagination that require a comprehensive suspension of disbelief. Examples: *Lord of The Rings*, anything by George R. R. Martin, *The Magicians*

Magical—stories about fantastical worlds with magical laws that can be mastered by certain beings, but not everyone. *Examples: Harry Potter* series, *and A Discovery of Witches*

Science Fiction—stories about the reaches of technology with an element of fantasy that allow the reader to suspend belief. Examples: *Ender's Game* and *The Martian*

Epistolary—stories built around letters. Example: *Letters from Juliette* and *The Perks of Being a Wallflower*.

Action—stories dealing with life and death. These novels tend to be recognized more by author than title. Examples: anything by Tom Clancy, Lee Childs, or Dan Brown.

Horror—stories where something worse than death is at stake, such as saving a soul from damnation. Examples: anything by Stephen King, the master of this genre

Crime—stories that deal with issues of justice. Examples: *Gone Girl* and *The Girl with the Dragon Tattoo*

Western—stories set west of the Rockies generally before the Industrial Revolution. Although modern westerns are possible.   Examples of westerns are *True Grit* and *Hour Glass* (Michelle Rene)

War—stories of courage, and might over right or right over might. Examples: *For Whom the Bell Tolls, The Things They Carried,* and *Unbroken*

Thriller—stories dealing with an aspect of evil or corruption that requires a hero to overcome. Examples: *The Girl on the Train* and *The Da Vinci Code*

Romance—stories dealing with love in all its forms, hate into love, finding love. Examples: *The Notebook* and anything else by Nicolas Sparks, *Me Before You* and *Pride and Prejudice.*

Classics – stories firmly engrained into the literary canon. You can't write a classic, a book becomes a classic. But it is important you know the distinction. Examples: *The Count of Monte Cristo, Jane Eyre, The Call of the Wild.*

Knowing your genre allows you to incorporate the conventions and obligatory scenes specific to your genre. For example, if you are writing a mystery, you will have a scene where the body is discovered, you may have a scene where you falsely accuse an innocent person, a scene where the murder is unveiled for the reader, and finally, a scene where justice is served. For more on obligatory scenes and conventions, I highly recommend *The Story Grid* by Shawn Coyne.

Scenes	Novels are built one scene at a time. Think of each scene as a self-contained story within your story with a beginning, middle and an ending. Writing scenes is a great way to up your writing game.

Resources

The Story Grid: What Good Editors Know by Shawn Coyne

Why I recommend it: First, *The Story Grid* is based on the experience of Shawn Coyne who was a sought-after editor at a number of big publishing houses before beginning his own imprint Black Irish Books with author Steven Pressfield. Over the years, Shawn developed a method for evaluating stories and helping writers see the gaps in their novels that he turned into *The Story Grid*.

Second, the method Shawn uses to analyze and build a story is the perfect follow up to *Your First Fifteen Pages*. I believe that if you use what you learn in this book for the beginning of your story and what Shawn teaches, you can develop a nearly perfect novel.

Chapter 2: Beginning with the Why

Without an inciting incident, nothing meaningful can happen. And when nothing meaningful happens, it's not a story.

—*Shawn Coyne, The Story Grid*

"I bought eggs," is not a story.

Even if we throw a few characters into the mix, and you tell me that you and James went to a farm stand to get fresh eggs on the way to my house and you bought them from the millennial chick with purple hair and a sleeve tattoo, who left her job at a nonprofit in DC to come back home and restart the family farm, it still isn't a story. It is a report. You bought eggs. James went with you. The millennial chick sold them to you at the stand on her family farm. So far, that isn't a story because there is nothing at stake for either the teller or the listener.

It's when we add the *why* – the reason for telling the story – that a report becomes a story.

> *"On the way here, I stopped at the farm stand that the millennial chick from DC runs, but she was out and . . .*
>
> *CC interrupted him, "Out of eggs or out, away from the stand?"*
>
> *"Wait," he puts up his hand. "Trust me, this gets good. This morning, around 6:00 when the millennial chick . . ."*
>
> *"Oh, so she was there. You have got to find out her name."*

James threw her a look. CC was always interrupting. "This morning, when the millennial chick, whose name I can't remember, was gathering eggs, four blacked out trucks with strange markings on the side pulled up. Some guys got out, flashed her badges, and told her they had to confiscate all the eggs."

"All of them?"

"Yep, every last one. The guys in the truck gave her a 'super legal looking document' and told her she had to surrender all her chickens too."

"Seriously? All her chickens? Are you making this shit up?" CC turned from the sink and wiped her hands. He'd finally gotten her attention.

"No. It gets even weirder. She told them to wait while she called the sheriff. But they didn't wait. By the time she came back outside, they had cleaned out all chickens and even taken all the straw from the coops and sprayed something blue in a ten-foot radius around the coops. After they left, she called around to other farms in the area, and found out the same thing is happening all across the state, as far south as Montgomery, she said."

James cocked his head toward the TV on the counter, "An unknown virus is spreading through chickens throughout the Southeast."

CC picked up the remote and turned up the volume. "The virus causes rapid breathing, chest pains, and headaches resulting in blindness. The symptoms mimic heart attacks or a stroke coming on very quickly and killing the infected person within hours of the first sign of pain or difficulty breathing. The virus is believed to have killed 37 people so far, and the count is expected to rise. Doctors at the CDC believe there is a link to the deaths and a virus found in chickens. Authorities are confiscating birds and eggs in Alabama, Mississippi, and Tennessee and expect they will have to eliminate more chickens before the virus is contained. If you have eggs in your refrigerator, we urge you to call the CDC immediately. We will scroll the number for the CDC throughout this broadcast."

James opened the fridge and peered in. There next to the milk and a half-eaten pie sat an ominous bowl of eggs. He picked up his phone and started dialing the number running along the bottom of the screen.

"Something about this isn't right," he said as he hit dial.

CC eyes lingered on his UAB hospital badge and the scrubs he wore on rounds.

Now, we have a story. A virus linked to chickens is killing people. A doctor who isn't buying the story. Developing, distinct characters. And we are asking – Why were the chickens taken and destroyed? How did the virus start? Is it killing everyone or just some people? What happens next? Will James be the one to figure this out?

We can begin to layer more detail onto this scene – place, time, and other specifics – but without the WHY of the virus, all the other details wouldn't matter. We simply have people talking about buying eggs.

Whether you are writing literary fiction or historical fiction, police procedural or YA, before readers can fully invest in reading your story, to get them past the first fifteen pages, you need to show them why they are reading. And before you begin to write, *you* need to have a clearly defined reason why you are writing the story you are writing. Are you exploring a story about a character who: takes the wrong job, finds a letter that upends their world, gives up her life for her sister, refuses to embrace slavery, or dies and is brought back to life? You need to know that before you begin writing.

In the case of the story about a virus and the eggs, perhaps the writer wants to explore what happens when a young doctor faces a killer virus. But to tell that story we have to have a place for the story to begin – unidentified men confiscating chickens and eggs in three states. Why? Because by having James tell us that story, we place the virus at the beginning of our novel. The why and the inciting incident become inextricably linked. As a writer, you need to know why you are telling the story you are telling. And why you started, where you did.

Once you have decided on the *why* – I want to tell a story about a killer virus and a young doctor – then you need a way into the story, an inciting incident that will allow you to build complications to move the story along. Once James becomes aware of the killer virus, we need a reason for him to move from believing that he is too inexperienced, too busy with work, or too removed from the situation to help – and see the moment he decides to take action.

There are multiple directions we can take this story. The phone could ring, and James' superior could call him back to the hospital. James could have a friend at the CDC who worked on the last bird flu, but when he calls him to find out what is going on, James discovers his friend is dead and was one of the first people to die from this new virus. CC could have eaten some of the eggs in the fridge, and by the next morning, she too could be dead, spurring James on to find the cure and the origin of this deadly virus. Where the story goes depends upon the inciting incident.

The inciting incident gives the reader and the writer a way into the story. It points to who has the most at stake. And most of the time, it will introduce us to the most important characters in the story.

Shawn Coyne, author of *The Story Grid*, puts it this way, "without an inciting incident, a writer has nothing…just a collection of riffs that don't add up in any coherent way…character sketches or meticulous Proustian descriptions of inanimate objects that have zero emotional payoff."

The Mistake of the Big Reveal

Often writers wait to reveal the inciting incident until later in the story thinking that by holding back, they keep the reader in suspense. Here's why holding back the inciting incident doesn't work. If your reader is still confused about what your story is about and isn't emotionally invested by page 15, or 20 or 25, most readers will stop reading and give up on your story.

Agents and editors make the decision to keep reading based on the first few pages of a manuscript. If we are three chapters in and still don't have a clue why we should care about a story, I guarantee we are moving on to the next manuscript and will not look back.

The big or slow reveal is an easy trap. Often writers think they can hold the reader's attention by making them wait for the big reveal. When you do this, you are confusing the inciting incident with the crisis of their story. The crisis comes in the middle of the story and leads to a turning point. The inciting incident is at the beginning of the story and kicks the story into gear.

How the Inciting Incident Works as Signpost

There are many schools of thought and books on writing. Some authors advocate the "just write" approach. Some authors encourage writers to write a "shitty first draft" and then worry about the story. Others advise, "don't edit, just write!"

But to write anything – a story, a report, even this book – you have to know *why* you are writing it. As a novelist, you have to hone in on the event that brought the story into being and why your reader should care. That *why* is the question at the heart of every novel.

Why read *Your First Fifteen Pages*? Because you want to develop a solid foundation for your novel and move beyond the agent's slush pile.

Why read *The Firm*? Because we've all had the experience of something sounding too good to be true and we want to know if this is one of those times.

Why read *The Husband's Secret*? Because we all know someone who's had a secret they didn't want revealed.

Why read *The Hunger Games*? Because we're curious about what it would be like to fight to the death, and if we would have the wherewithal to survive.

Why read *Harry Potter*? Because we want to believe magic exists, and see good triumph over evil.

Why read *The Invention of Wings*? Because we are still trying to wrap our heads around slavery, why it lasted for as long as it did, and what finally brought about its demise.

There are a million other reasons why we read fiction. Here are just a few more: Because we want to know what it is like to be a spy, fight for someone's freedom, discover a treasure, change identities, fail and finally succeed, come back to life...the list goes on and on.

For many writers, the *why* of a story comes from a place of natural curiosity. Before Liane Moriarty wrote *The Husband's Secret*, she stumbled upon an article about deathbed confessions ranging from a man who faked a picture of the Loch Ness monster, to a famous songwriter who plagiarized a hit song and lied about it for years. But the confession that "got me thinking," Moriarty writes, was the man who confessed to murdering his neighbor after having a stroke. The man didn't die, but the secret he almost carried to the grave was out. That was the germ of the idea for The Husband's Secret, "a deathbed confession, except he's not dead. Years later, after his wife finds the letter, she faces an interesting ethical dilemma."

Finding this explanation for the genesis of Moriarty's story on the Kindle version of *The Husband's Secret* was an unexpected gift. Unless we attend author readings or conferences or come across an article by someone savvy enough to ask "Where did you come up with the idea for your novel," we aren't often privy to the ways writers get their ideas. We seldom know where the germ of a novel comes from and how it goes from idea to fully formed book.

Fortunately, in the case of Moriarty, we do. We know that she read an article on deathbed confessions and that ideas wriggled around in her subconscious until she began to layer characters, place, and complications on top of the original premise.

In *The Husband's Secret*, the inciting incident is the discovery of the letter with "For my wife, Cecilia Fitzpatrick. To be opened only in the event of my death" written on it. From that point on, everything in the novel supports the finding of the envelope. The decision to open it or not open it. The decision to tell her husband, John Paul, she'd found the envelope. The opening of the envelope by Cecilia. The consequences that follow. Each character and that character's actions, *everything* he or she does, ties directly back to finding the envelope. As we read *The Husband's Secret,* every action Cecilia and the characters around her take move us towards the final resolution – why John Paul wrote the letter in the first place.

Strong plots build from the inciting incident to the ultimate resolution of the story. A great story takes us from a question – why did Cecilia's husband write a letter to be opened only after his death? To the inciting incident – Cecilia finding the letter. To a stunning revelation at the end of the novel – *which I won't spoil for you!* Every scene, character, action, complication, and plot twist in *The Husband's Secret* leads us, like Hansel and Gretel's breadcrumbs, from the inciting incident to that revelation.

Having a fully formed inciting incident at the beginning of your book, knowing why you are writing the story and what your inciting incident is, helps you keep the story on track as you write. If you find yourself writing a scene in chapter 12 of your book and you suddenly have no idea where you are going, go back to the inciting incident of the book and ask yourself, "Does this scene support the *why*?" If not, retrace your steps back until you see where the story diverged from that first inciting event.

Let's go back to the story about the woman on the train from Chapter 1 for a moment. As the writer, you might decide to take her back to the auction house where she works. We see her doing her job, interacting with coworkers and clients. At some point in the day, she receives a package. When she opens it, she finds a child's doll wearing a faded dress that looks familiar, but she can't seem to place it. Later in the story, we realize the material of the dress and the backpack is the same, and the mystery man on the train sent her the doll. She realizes he knows who she is and where she works. This scene supports why we are interested in the story. We want to find out who the mysterious guy with the backpack is, and we want to know what is up with that backpack. Did he steal it? Did he murder a little girl? If so, why would he hang on to it? How did he find her?

But, let's say that rather than writing a scene about receiving the doll, you write a scene that is just about the woman on the train at her office. Without the complication of the doll, we lose interest in the story. After a few more disconnected scenes that move us further and further from the inciting incident, we start to wonder where the story is going, and we stop reading.

This is so important I will repeat it yet again. Every scene, every complication (the doll), every character, and every action ultimately needs to tie back to your *why* and the inciting incident.

If you haven't defined the *why* of your story and your inciting incident isn't in the first fifteen pages, you'll be stuck, wandering around in a writing desert and dragging your reader along with you.

I participate in a Wednesday co-writing group. Every Wednesday we get together and work on each other's stories. Half of the writers in the group have been working on their novels for years the other half is just beginning. All are struggling with identifying their inciting incident. Emily has been working on her book for years. She's written multiple drafts. She's signed up for numerous workshops, and yet, she's still plugging away on her novel. Lisa has the idea for a compelling dark comedy about a creepy neighbor. Her characters are captivating and the basic outline of the story interesting, but we still haven't nailed a strong inciting incident down that allows the story to build the way she wants. Nailing that inciting incident is key to everything that comes after. It will keep you from working through endless drafts and a novel for years without finishing. And it will help you get past the first fifteen pages on solid footing.

Let's run through a few more examples before you tackle the why and the inciting incident for your story.

The Firm opens with a young lawyer, Mitch McDeere, interviewing for his first job out of law school. The inciting incident comes on page 13. After hearing everything that Bendini, Lambert, & Locke, a small firm in Memphis, Tennessee is offering, Mitch's wife Abby says, "I don't understand Mitch. Why are they so generous?" And off the story goes! The theme is, if something is too good to be true it probably is. Everything in *The Firm* points to that theme and back to the question "Why is this small firm in Memphis (few people have heard of) being so generous?" By the time Mitch figures out why, we are hooked! We keep reading to see how he will extricate himself and his career from the firm.

The Martian opens with Mark Watley injured and left for dead on Mars. He must figure out a way to survive until the next team arrives on the planet *in four years*. He has enough food to last one year if he rations it. He can either give up and die or find a way to grow food and survive. After Watley explains his dilemma to us, and we see him moving from analysis to survival mode, we are on board. From that point on, everything in the novel is about Watley surviving until he is rescued.

The Invention of Wings begins on Sarah Grimke's eleventh birthday. For her birthday, Sarah's mother presents her with the gift of a young slave girl Handful. Everything in Sarah rebels against accepting another human being as a gift and everything in *The Invention of Wings* points back to the internal struggle against slavery, and of being enslaved, lived through the characters of Sarah and Handful.

The Hunger Games – Katniss prepares for the Reaping, a ceremony during which a representative from each district chooses two tributes to participate in an annual fight to the death called the Hunger Games. When the representative selects her sister Prim, Katniss steps in to take Prim's place. Each action, decision, and complication is tied to Katniss' promise to stay alive and return to her family.

Now it's your turn.

Your First 15

Why should we read your story? What will we learn? Where does your story begin?

Take some time and focus on your story. What was the impetus? What is the theme of the story? *What is the inciting incident?*

For a new story, identify:

1. The idea that inspired the story.

2. The overall theme of your story.

3. Your genre.

4. The inciting incident – the event that kicks off the story.

5. Your reader. Who do you hope to move, impact, or entertain with your story?

For an existing story, identify:

1. The idea that inspired your story.

2. The overall theme of your story.

3. The inciting incident – the event that kicks off the story and the page number where the incident occurs.

4. Your reader. Who do you hope to move, impact, or entertain with your story?

Determine if:

1. The inciting incident appears in the first 15 pages of your story.

2. The main character is introduced before page 15.

3. How you can move the inciting incident up if it doesn't occur before page 15.

4. The inciting incident allows you to effectively build the remainder of your story or if you need to begin again with a new inciting incident that will serve as a stronger anchor for the rest of your novel.

Resources

Christopher Vogler, *The Writer's Journey: Mythical Structure for Writers*

Why I recommend it: Vogler does a great job of taking the Hero's Journey that Joseph Campbell laid out in *The Hero with a Thousand Faces* and showing how it can be used as the basis for a story. *The Writer's Journey* offers a helpful structure if you are writing a redemption story, an adventure where one or more character changes significantly over the course of the novel, or even a romance where the protagonist faces numerous obstacles before being united or reunited with their true love.

The hero's journey begins in the Ordinary World and ends when the hero Returns with the Elixir. The chart below shows the stages of the hero's journey:

THE HERO'S JOURNEY

I encourage you to explore *The Writer's Journey*. It is a short read. I also encourage you to apply the parts of the hero's journey that work for your story and to discard the rest.

The hero's/writer's journey is a tool you should be familiar with and have at your fingertips, especially if you are writing fantasy or coming of age. Writers often bandy about the terminology of the hero's journey. Becoming familiar with it allows you to participate in the conversation when someone tells you who the trickster or the shape-shifter is in their story or asks when the seizing of the sword occurs in yours.

The most frustrating submissions we get are those that have obviously tried to force every element of the hero's journey model into a story. Not every story will have a mentor appear in exactly the way Vogler prescribes. Just as all the archetypes Vogler discusses don't appear in every story. Use tools such as the hero's journey as a guide not an absolute.

Chapter 3: The Players

"When writing a novel a writer should create living people; people, not characters. A character is a caricature."

—*Ernest Hemingway*

Characters, major and minor, serve one specific function – they move the story along through action and dialogue. Without at least one character, there is no story. You can create the most detailed, intricate setting. You can have a compelling theme – survival against all odds. You can have an incredible inciting incident – a dust storm on Mars. But, if you don't have a character or two, there is no story.

Without Mark Watley, *The Martian* would be a book about scientific equipment destroyed by a dust storm. To tell the story of surviving, against-all-odds, author Andy Weir needed to give his reader someone to champion. A character that would face monumental odds, give up when things seemed hopeless, then (because humans are wired to survive) come up with an idea that might work or might not, but was worth a try. He needed a character that believed trying was better than dying alone on a desolate planet. A character that would have small victories and significant setbacks and face an ultimate all hope is lost moment, before being rescued by a crew that never gave up trying to get back to him once they knew he was alive.

Without Mark Watley and the other characters in *The Martian*, we wouldn't have the series of actions, decisions, dialogue, and complications that come from people interacting with one another, making mistakes, or doing the right thing that makes a novel, a novel.

On the first page of *The Martian*, we learn Mark Watley is "fucked." And, he is the only person who will die on Mars. A few pages later, we learn he is the junior crewmember on a mission to Mars left for dead by his crew after a dust storm nearly destroyed their only way off the planet. We learn that Watley isn't the type of person to roll over and die after we see him giving himself stitches. We learn he isn't a person who gives in to panic. After patching himself up, he calmly assesses his situation. Within days of being abandoned, he has a plan for survival. We learn he is a botanist and he comes up with a plan to grow food. By page 15, we are rooting for Watley.

In *The Martian*, Watley is the story – what he thinks, what he does, how he survives mentally and physically – that is the story. Weir gives us glimpses of the crew and NASA and the ground crew who sent him to Mars, but the story of survival against all odds is Watley's to tell. By not introducing us to more people in those first fifteen pages, Weir creates an intimate relationship between his main character and the reader and emphasizes that this is Watley's story. We feel his isolation, and we want him to survive.

The First Fifteen Pages Party

Have you ever been to a party with a friend who knows everyone and insists on introducing you to everyone there? You spend the evening meeting person after person, "Oh there's John, you have to meet him," only to have your friend pull you away to meet Alicia, and then Brent, and then Eloise, until they all become a blur.

A few days later, your friend is waxing poetic about what a great time she had and she starts quizzing you about the people you met. "Don't you just love Alicia? Her work is amazing."

"Really?" you ask, trying to conjure up an image of Alicia. "What does she do?"

"What do you mean what does she do? I introduced you to her so you could talk about her work. The two of you have so much in common!"

Don't be that person. Don't be the writer who introduces the reader to everyone in the story within the first fifteen or so pages. Don't create a big dinner party at the beginning of your novel that leaves us wondering who the characters are and what their roles are in the story.

The first fifteen pages should introduce the reader to the main characters, the people we need to get to know to become invested in your story. And only introduce us to the characters directly impacted by your inciting incident. Otherwise, you are setting up your reader for confusion and disappointment.

Also, don't be the person who lures us to dinner with the hint of someone we can't wait to meet joining us and then tell us once we get there they aren't coming. How does this apply to writing? I recently read a submission that began with a prologue about an elderly couple living quietly in Poland in the midst of World War II. In his prologue, the writer did a brilliant job of situating the reader in time and place and creating a beautiful character sketch of an elderly couple living in the country that had, until that point, avoided the war. Within a few short pages, I fell in love with the couple. I wanted to know what was going to happen to them. And then the writer did the unthinkable. He killed them off, just as we were getting to know them. While the author attempted to use the prologue to draw the reader in by showing us the level of brutality embraced by the recurring characters, for me, it was unsuccessful. The other characters in those first fifteen pages were stereotypes or too remote. All I could think about as I read the rest of the submission were the old man and his wife lying dead outside their home. Rather than keep reading, for me, the story was over before it got rolling.

A note on killing your darlings: There are times when killing off your reader's favorite character works. Serial TV relies heavily on this device. The immensely popular "Game of Thrones" series is a perfect example. George R.R. Martin spends a good bit of time developing a character, and then just when the audience is fully invested and loves the character, Martin kills them off as a transition to the next big idea or season. BUT, he only uses this option when he knows that the audience has become invested in another character that he has developed to take the place of the character he is killing off. For example, no one would have rooted for Jon Snow as much as they did if he wasn't the last male Stark, and he wouldn't be the last male Stark if the writer hadn't beheaded his father in the first season, or killed Rob off during the Red Wedding in season three. Jon Snow's character was created to embody all the positive traits of the Starks, and to learn from their mistakes. Jon isn't trusting like Ned, he isn't vain or arrogant like Rob, nor does he allow women to distract him from his duty. If you are going to kill off an established character, have someone waiting in the wings to pick up the reader's interest and loyalty.

Think of your opening pages as an intimate dinner party for two or four or maybe six if you are adept at entertaining and can pull it off. You've invited these people to your table because they know things we, the reader, need to know, perspectives we need to understand, and have information to impart that ties directly to the inciting incident. Otherwise, they might as well be a chair or a candlestick, not a character.

In many of the opening pages we read, either the characters or their motivations are obscure, leaving us wondering what the story is about. Your first fifteen pages should:

1. Introduce the main characters in the novel. If the story is primarily about the actions or journey of one character, focus on that character in those first pages. You can give us glimpses of other characters but don't try to introduce everyone in the first few pages if they are not integral to either the inciting incident or to the overall plot.

2. Include unique details and distinguishing traits for each character you introduce to encourage your reader to begin a relationship with the people in your story.

3. Infuse each character introduced in the first fifteen pages with action, dialogue, and purpose. Remember a character is there for one purpose – to advance the story. Period. If a character doesn't advance the story through dialogue or action, they shouldn't be in your novel.

Establishing Characters

At the risk of extending the metaphor a bit too far, think about what it is like to sit at dinner next to someone who offers very little in the way of meaningful conversation. When we encounter someone who answers a question with one or two-word answers or doesn't offer enough details to keep the conversation moving, we turn to the person on our other side hoping for a better dinner partner.

The same is true of characters in your story. When we encounter a character in your novel, we want to know who they are, what makes them tick and most importantly, we want to know why they are in the story. We want to see how they are relevant to the plot and feel as if they aren't wasting our precious time.

Let's look at an example. *The Husband's Secret* opens with Cecilia sitting at her kitchen table contemplating a letter she found while looking for a piece of the Berlin Wall. In the first fifteen pages, we learn that Cecilia is "the most decisive person she knows," and that she is a woman with close relationships, some of which, she values more than others. We learn she is meticulous because "she cleaned the droplets of water in the kitchen sink with a paper towel until it shone." We know that she is a practicing Catholic who has given up wine for Lent, which gives us a hint about where she stands morally. She is the person who hosts all the major events and holidays for her family. And, we find out that she is a "meticulous planner."

Moriarty reveals that she is the mother of three pre-teen daughters, who Cecilia worries are becoming too body conscious. We learn that she is school mum and a part-time Tupperware consultant. We know that a year ago Cecilia witnessed a child on his way to school in a Spiderman costume get hit by a car. And we know that horrific event has played over in her mind "a thousand times."

By the end of the first fifteen pages, we know Cecilia is a talker and that "silence doesn't come naturally" to her. We know that as a young woman, she traveled to Berlin just as the wall was coming down and she brought a small piece back as a souvenir. We know that her being there at that time in history was a fluke. Then as now, she has never been a "curious, politically aware" person. We know this because she asks her daughter Esther about the Berlin Wall rather than look it up or read about it herself. Cecilia is a woman on the go, someone who "doesn't normally sit down in the mornings." Someone who, "generally, ate her breakfast standing at the counter, while she made lunches, checked her Tupperware orders on her iPad, unpacked the dishwasher, and texted clients about parties." And from that sentence alone, we know that she is a deliberate person with a busy, orderly life.

All of these details are vital for us to understand why finding the letter creates a crisis, a turning point in Cecilia's life. If she were a flighty person given to impulse, she would have ripped open the envelope, and the story would be over. For the story to move forward, we have to understand who Cecilia is. We have to know that she doesn't act hastily without thought. We have to see Cecilia as a person who respects boundaries and privacy. We have to get that she is obsessively organized and doesn't tolerate mess or loose ends. She is a person who has gone to great lengths to ensure that her life stays on track and that there are no surprises.

Who Cecilia is, is imperative to the main *what* of those first fifteen pages. By the end of those first fifteen pages, we want to know what Cecilia will do – will she or won't she open the letter? Moriarty knows that by giving us a detailed character sketch of Cecilia we start to relate to her, and we become curious about what she will do next. Even if we aren't as meticulous as Cecilia, or living lives as well ordered, we can all relate to having things be perfect one minute and then having something come along the next that changes everything. By making Cecilia a fully developed character, we trust her to tell us her story.

Far too often, we receive submissions with flat, undefined, one-dimensional characters. The writers of these submissions spend a good bit of time reporting, ticking off information about their characters, rather than showing us through tight, thick details or actions who they are. For example, the main character in a submission I read this morning was described as a "relatively tall man," "slender," and "handsome enough." The writer spent more time drawing a vivid picture of the cows in the scene than the characters. By page three, I had to force myself to read the rest of the submission. The writer introduced six characters in the first fifteen pages, one was merely a glimpse, but according to the writer's query, she was a pivotal character. Beyond knowing that one character was tall, slender and moderately handsome, I couldn't tell you a thing about anyone in her story. For me, her first fifteen pages did not help establish a relationship with any of the characters. By the end of those crucial first fifteen pages, I wasn't invested enough to want to know more about anyone in the story, except maybe the cows. Rather than request a full manuscript, I sent the writer a pass with love email.

One of the big goals of your first fifteen pages is to make us fall in love with, hate, or be so curious about one or two of your characters we keep reading. Your characters should make us want to know what happens next. To do that, you have to show us who those characters are.

Creating Layered Characters

Consider the things we might need to know about your character. The identity markers that fit within the story and help create an engaging and layered character. Here are some identity markers to consider:

- age

- profession

- physical characteristics

- social standing – class, schooling, neighborhood

- emotional state at the beginning of the novel

- beliefs

- opinions

- unique markers – magical ability, terminal illness, runaway, murderer

- virtues – kind, forgiving, funny, creative, open-minded

- vices – angry, abusive, lies, manipulative

If a marker isn't relevant to your story, don't spend time describing it to the reader. For example, in *Harry Potter and the Sorcerer's Stone,* we don't know the marital status of Professor McGonagall or of many of the other characters in the novel. Children are not interested in whether or not a character is married or to whom they are married unless there is a reason to tell them. We know that Ron's parents are married and they seem to have a loving relationship. This information is useful because it sets up Harry's twinges of envy when he visits Ron's home, reminding him he is an orphan.

In *The Firm*, knowing about Mitch's physical appearance is not as necessary as understanding his values, work ethic, knowledge of the law, and intelligence. Grisham doesn't bore his reader with a lengthy description of Mitch. It doesn't matter to the story if he's tall or short, thin or pudgy, has blond or dark hair. He's a law student looking for his first job. He's hungry. He's smart. Grisham develops these identity markers because they have a direct bearing on the story.

Far too many of the submissions we read present one-dimensional characters. Rather than a hungry lawyer from a broken home who has worked hard to overcome poverty, loves his wife, and still believes in the American Dream, a writer might give us a stereotypically angry young man who hates the world and offers him no opportunity for redemption.

A Cautionary Tale	In 2016, a publisher released a book to too much fanfare and reviews. The hype around this book was incredible, partly due to the reportedly million-dollar advance the author received.
	The reader reviews were a mixed bag. Ranging from "I loved it!" to "I couldn't finish it" to "I wish there was a way to get back the time I spent reading it and the money I paid for it!" Overwhelmingly, the biggest complaint about the book, there wasn't one character out of a very large cast that most readers related to or could root for. Not one.
	If you want more positive reviews than negative, give us someone to like, someone relatable, someone to root for!

Avoiding One Dimensional Characters

People are rarely all good or all bad. We are a layering of our political, social, economic, family, educational, religious, and ethnic experiences. We have virtues and vices. But we don't bring everything that makes us who we are to every situation we encounter. There are times when our politics don't matter, or our education might not come into play. At a dinner party, we might or might not talk about the time we met the Dalai Lama, or we might share the time we hung out with Willie Nelson. What we choose to share depends on the circumstances – the story we are telling, the people listening, the event, and the setting.

The same is true of the characters in your story. Create the layers you need for each character in your novel. Put in the identity markers that are important to the story and leave out the rest. Give your characters an exciting or funny quirk by adding a marker or two that makes them unique. And above all, *show don't tell*.

Show Don't Tell

Consider the difference between "she cleaned the droplets of water in the kitchen sink with a paper towel until it shone," and she was "obsessive compulsive." The first description is an example of showing. We can picture someone with a paper towel buffing the sink to a high sheen. The second description is an example of telling – we cannot see obsessive-compulsive, not unless we've known a truly obsessive-compulsive person.

We cannot see "he was impatient." We can see "he swung his keys around and around his finger, pacing in front of the restaurant, waiting for her to show up."

Rather than tell us that Katniss is a rule breaker who will do anything to feed her family in *The Hunger Games*, Suzanne Collins shows us. For example, after telling us about the fence surrounding District 12 and why it is there, Collins shows us essential aspects of who Katniss is. After "taking a moment to listen carefully for the hum that means the fence is live" she flattens on her belly behind a clump of bushes to "slide under a two-foot stretch that's been loose for years." Once in the trees, Katniss retrieves "a bow and sheath of arrows from a hollow log." When we see her retrieving the bow and arrows, we see her as a hunter. This seemingly small detail introduced on page three will grow into a powerful image of Katniss as the story progresses.

Telling is fine to impart information. For example, Collins tells us that "trespassing in the woods is illegal, and poaching carries the severest of penalties," but more people would do it if they had a weapon, which is also illegal.

By showing us the bow and arrow and then telling us that being in the woods and poaching is illegal, we begin to form a picture of a bold, brave young woman who is willing to risk punishment to feed her family. Every detail, every distinction made between Katniss and Gale, between Katniss and her mother and between Katniss and Prim in those crucial first pages show that Katniss is willing to sacrifice anything for the sake of her family. Without that understanding, what happens next in the novel would make little sense to the reader. Everything that comes after the first chapter reflects the person and the theme Collins establishes in those first fifteen pages. From start to finish, this is a story about a brave and fearless young woman who will do anything to keep her family, and primarily her younger sister, safe.

Let's look at one more example of showing versus telling. When Sue Monk Kidd introduces us to Handful, one of the young girls at the heart of *The Invention of Wings*, she begins with a story passed down from mother to daughter about the time in Africa when people could fly. Her mother rubs the nubs of her shoulder blades telling Handful that this is where her wings used to be. Through the telling of this story, in just a few short paragraphs, Kidd provides us with a series of distinct character markers. Handful is a slave, and she is close to her mother. At ten, she is too "shrewd" to believe in fairy tales or magic, and she can read and write. All of these character traits are crucial to the development of Handful's character.

We meet Sarah, the other main character, on the morning of her eleventh birthday as she is leaving behind the "porcelain dolls and teacups" of the nursery for her own room. We learn that she isn't as fearless as everyone believes. Rather she likens herself to a tortoise. She would rather hide than confront anything fearful that crosses her path. She is pampered and comes from a wealthy family. We know this because Kidd shows us Sarah's "nursery mauma," who is busy putting away Sarah's things in her wardrobe while downstairs her Mother had "slaves pulling out Chinese tureens and Wedgewood cups" for her birthday party.

Kidd provides us with the portrait of two young girls, who on the surface appear to be very different. One is white, one black. One is a slave, the other free. One appears poor, while the other seems surrounded by wealth. What we find as the novel unfolds is that none of us is ever completely free or completely enslaved. That wealth does not provide salve for the soul. And poverty can be a state of mind. Our sympathies flip from one child to the next, from one young woman to the other as the characters grow together, then apart, and are reunited. But for the reader to get to Kidd's masterful ending, we have to want to know more about Handful and Sarah. We have to be emotionally invested to keep reading.

What's in a Name?

When I was a young writer, I had the opportunity to have coffee with my first author crush, T.R. Pearson. One of the first questions I asked him was how he came up with the names for his characters. Pearson's books were rich southern gothic tales set in the heart of Dixie and his names Everett Little, Aunt Willa, and Grandma Yount reflected the richness of the culture. So too did the use of both first and last names throughout the story. For example, Everett Little isn't introduced as Evertt Little and then later referred to as only Everett. He remains Evertt Little throughout the novel because in the South some people are both their first *and* last names. Aunt Willa could have been Aunt Sue or Aunt Ann, but Willa depicts a wistfulness associated with the South.

Names matter. They help us envision your character.

Pearson told me when he was starting a new book he went to the cemetery and walked through the graves, combining the first name from one stone with the last name of another. Mixing and matching until he had the character's name exactly right.

There is nothing worse than reading a submission and getting tripped up by the names the author has given to the characters, especially where there doesn't seem to be any reason for giving a character a distinctly tricky or unusual name. Writers do this quite often in period pieces and works set in other countries.

Names are significant. Your characters' names should add to our understanding of each character, not confuse us or cause the reader to stop and work to figure out a name if there is no reason for it to be unique or obtuse. The flipside of the naming dilemma is attaching a common name to a character that should have a unique name, especially if that character inhabits a world the author has created.

When deciding on the names of the characters in *The Hunger Games,* Suzanne Collins used a naming scheme that, while not obvious, becomes brilliant once we know about it. For the names of those living in the districts, she chose to use plant and nature-based names – Primrose, Katniss, Rue, Hawthorn. For those living in the ruling capital, she used names with a Roman influence – Seneca, Effie, Claudius. If you'd like to read more about her naming scheme, you can find the Slate magazine article on yourfirstfifteenpages.com under Resources.

The names in *The Hunger Games* work so well because Collins understood that the names she gave her characters would help define the world she was creating. The same is true of the naming scheme devised by Rowling for the *Harry Potter* series. When the books open, Harry, Hermione, and Ron are regular kids, who are later forced to confront evil. Their names allow any child to relate to the characters. By choosing names that were outside mainstream reference for other characters, Rowling signals that these people are different and inhabit a different realm. The names Hagrid, Dumbledore, Snape, and of course Voldemort, conjure up curiosity about who these people are.

Choose your character names wisely. Do you want us to relate to your character? To feel empathy? To be repulsed by them? Choose names that evoke the feeling you want your reader to have for that character. Don't choose a name just to be different or controversial if that isn't the role the character plays in the story. Names matter.

Objects as Characters

Occasionally, you will come across an object in a novel that becomes a focus of the story. In *The Husband's Secret*, this happens with the envelope Cecilia finds. The envelope takes on such importance that it becomes a character. Rather than say she found an envelope, she offers a thick description of it, telling her reader:

> *"The envelope was gray with a fine layer of dust. The words on the front were written in a scratchy blue ballpoint pen, the handwriting as familiar as her own. She turned it over. It was sealed with a yellowing piece of sticky tape. When was it written? It felt old like it had been written years ago, but there was no way of knowing for sure."*

As the story unfolds, the envelope becomes a presence. It is with Cecilia even when she is out, and the envelope is at home. Its contents weigh on her, causing her dread, shame, anguish. The secret contained within, too heavy a burden for her to bear.

Without the envelope, we wouldn't have an inciting incident. The envelope becomes the focus of the story, and because it does, it shares the spotlight with Cecilia becoming a character in the story.

We could also make the case that in *The Firm*, the firm itself becomes a character. Although Grisham develops characters to represent the firm and we see these characters throughout the book, the battle for Mitch to get his life back is with the firm. The inciting incident is Mitch taking a job with a firm that seems too good to be true. He doesn't take a job with Lamar Quinn or Oliver Lambert. He takes a job with the firm.

Your First 15

Think about your own first fifteen pages. Who does the reader meet in your opening chapter(s)? Who appears on stage from the beginning? Are these the people we need to get to know early in your story to become engaged in your novel? Have you given us someone to root for? Have you left a critical character out?

For a new story, identify:

1. The characters in your story.

2. The protagonist of your story – the main character.

3. Who does the reader need to meet in the first fifteen pages?

For an existing story, identify:

1. The characters in your story.

2. The characters that appear in the story from the beginning.

3. If these are the people the reader needs to meet early on in the story?

AND, determine if:

1. You need to change point of view.

2. You need to introduce the main character sooner.

3. You are developing your characters distinctly enough for your reader.

Resources

The Writer's Guide to Character Traits by Dr. Linda Edelstein.

The Positive Trait Thesaurus: A Writer's Guide to Character Attributes by Angela Ackerman and Becca Puglisi

The Negative Trait Thesaurus: A Writer's Guide to Character Flaws by Angela Ackerman and Becca Puglisi

Why I recommend these: Having one or two of these books at your disposal will help you define and layer your characters. If you are struggling with a protagonist who is overly cautious in relationships, but you aren't sure how to describe this trait, look up cautious in *The Positive Trait Thesaurus*.

Some possible ways to describe your character's behavior might be:

* closed body language

* overdoing research into a person or an event

* the need to go over details again and again.

You *could* spend hours trying to describe your character's behavior, or you could look it up and then write a description of the behavior that fits perfectly with your character and the story.

Chapter 4: Point of View

You never really understand a person until you consider things from his point of view.

—*Harper Lee*

Deciding who is telling your story and the point of view of that character are critical decision points for your story. As the writer, you determine how close the reader needs to be to the main characters. Do we need to be inside their heads? Or, would the reader be better positioned outside the head of any one character?

There are advantages to both first person and third person points of view.

First Person

First person point of view draws the reader into an intimate relationship with one character. If you have one character that is central to the story, and without that character, there would be no story, choosing the first person point of view might make sense. Writing in first person means, your protagonist, the main character in your novel, drives the story. And, that character should go through significant growth and change during the story.

First person keeps the reader in suspense because we only know what the main character knows. And, what the character tells us reveals what we need to know about them and the other characters in the story.

Let's look at an example from *The Hunger Games:*

> *"Hey, Catnip," says Gale. My real name is Katniss, but when I first told him, I had barely whispered it. So he thought I'd said Catnip. Then when this crazy lynx started following me around the woods looking for handouts, it became his official name for me. I finally had to kill the lynx because he scared off the game. I almost regretted it because he wasn't bad company. But I got a decent price for the pelt."*

This bit of internal dialogue comes on page 7. This exchange, from Katniss' point of view about her relationship with Gale, is both telling and necessary for the development of the story. The tension between Gale and Katniss is revealed later, but for now, Katniss and the reader are unaware of his feelings, because she is still in denial of hers.

The Hunger Games is Katniss' story to tell. Collins could have chosen to tell the story in third person, but that perspective may have shifted the reader's loyalty away from Katniss to other characters and Collins wanted her reader to root for Katniss. Telling her story in first person makes sense.

The same is true of *The Martian.* The story is Watley's to tell. And much of what he tells comes from the log he is keeping. While the story could have been told from third person the reader, might have lost some of the intimacy that a first person point of view provides.

Avoiding the Traps of First Person Point of View

If we aren't careful, writing in first person can lead us into two traps. Let's discuss both so that you can avoid these pitfalls in your novel.

1. *The Seagull effect* – We've all known seagulls, the person who talks about themselves incessantly, mimicking the "ey, ey, ey" cry of a seagull. Their talk is littered with *I*s – I went, I did, I ate, I said, I know. If the writer isn't careful, writing in first person can take on the seagull persona. Rather than developing an intimacy with the reader, the *I*s begin to irritate us, causing us to stop reading.

To avoid this trap in *The Martin,* Weir begins a paragraph with "I guess I should explain how Mars missions work." He then switches to "we" and proceeds to explain the ins and outs of mission development before switching briefly to second person, "You'd be amazed at how fast you can get going with a tiny acceleration over a long time." Occasionally adding a "we" and "you" into the narrative breaks up the "ey ey ey" seagull effect. It keeps the narration conversational. Watley is talking directly to us, the reader, because for a major portion of the book, the imaginary reader of his log is all the company he has.

2. *Hogging the Spotlight effect* – We've all known people who hog the spotlight even though the emphasis should be on the ensemble. When you are writing a novel that focuses on more than one character, and at least two of your characters will change and evolve because of their interactions with others, telling the story from first person may not be the best choice. While J. K. Rowling could have used first person for her *Harry Potter* series, telling the story strictly from Harry's "I" point of view would have diminished the changes Ron and Hermione go through in each story and from book one to the last book in the series. Using third person allowed Rowling to shift from Harry's to Ron's to Hermione's perspective and lets the reader root for the ensemble, rather than just Harry.

To avoid this trap determine if this is a story about the growth of one character or if multiple characters grow and change throughout your story. Do you want the reader rooting for one person or multiple people? Switch points of view if you have a character hogging the spotlight unnecessarily.

Third Person

Third person point of view places the reader in the room with the characters, rather than in the head of a specific character. It allows us to see the action as if we are flies on the wall in the room hearing what others might think and seeing the action others are seeing. As opposed to first person, which limits the reader's knowledge to only the things the main character knows, third person opens up to information from all the characters. And choosing the third person point of view means the actions of anyone in the ensemble can and will drive the story at any given time.

Third person works best when there is information the main character isn't privy to, but the reader needs to know. While many writing teachers and books suggest new writers write in first person, I advocate trying your hand at third person. I find it easier to tell a story when all the information and action isn't focused on one person in the story. And, it gives your reader additional characters to empathize with and root for.

Second Person

Jay McInerney's debut novel *Bright Lights, Big City*, was considered a tour de force when it came out in 1986. McInerney burst on the literary scene with a "generation-defining" book written in second person. Here's an excerpt:

> *You have traveled the course of the night from the meticulous to the slime. The girl with the shaved head has a scar tattooed on her scalp. It looks like a long, sutured gash. You tell her it is very realistic. She takes this as a compliment and thanks you. You meant as opposed to romantic.*

The "you" point of view in *Bright Lights, Big City*, was used to put the reader not just in the head of the narrator, but have the reader look through his eyes and see what was going on as if the action was happening directly to *you*, the reader. Using the second person point of view was McInerney telling the reader "imagine if you were me and you were living in New York in the mid-1980s, you would . . ." By employing this point of view, people living in Des Moines or Birmingham or Oklahoma City could live vicariously through Jay McInerney. This point of view invites us to imagine we are there, walking the streets of New York, casually conversing with the tattooed girl and seeing it all through our own eyes.

There is a pitfall to second person point of view. Like the *I* of first person point of view, the *you* of second person point of view can begin to pile up leaving us wondering who is talking and wondering why we should care.

Second person point of view is incredibly difficult to pull off. It is used when the writer needs the reader to feel as if they are *living* the experience the writer is portraying first hand. There needs to be a good reason for telling a story in second person, for putting the character in the shoes, rather than in the head of or the room with your characters. Otherwise, second person point of view can come off as gimmicky rather than effective.

Shifting Point of View

Shifting point of view allows the narration to fall with different characters throughout the story. This point of view works best when we need to get specific information from a specific character. For example, in *The Invention of Wings*, Kidd shifts the narrative from Handful to Sarah in alternating chapters. As the story unfolds, Sarah's perspective follows Handful's description of events, creating a complex account of slavery and enslavement. Both Handful and Sarah tell their story in first person. However, as the chapters alternate, Kidd shifts the point of view from one girl to the other keeping the intimacy of the first person narrative, allowing both characters to share the spotlight.

In *The Husband's Secret*, Moriarty uses third person narrative to provide the reader with information as either Cecilia or later Rachael Crowley discovers it. Moriarty could have told the story in first person from Cecilia's point of view, but she knew the reader needed distance to understand what each character has at stake in the story. While this is primarily Cecilia's story, the change Rachael goes through is also crucial to the story. Shifting the point of view from Cecilia and then Rachael shows us how events affect different people in profoundly different ways. We might not have gotten that insight using the first person point of view.

Your First 15

For a new story, identify:

1. The best point of view for your story. Try writing your opening scenes in first person and then, third person. Shift the narration from one character to another until you feel you have the point of view nailed down for your story.

For an existing story, identify:

1. The current point of view of your story.

2. If you are using the most effective point of view. Try rewriting your opening scenes in first person and then third person. Shift the narration from one character to another until you feel you have the point of view nailed down for your story.

Resources

I recently came across an interview with the director of *The Hunger Games* movie Gary Ross explaining his decision to film the movie using the point of view he chose.

Read the book, then watch the movie, then read the interview.

Consider the decision on point of view Suzanne Collins made. Do you agree or disagree with the choices Gary Ross made? After reading the interview did you change your mind or would you have chosen a different point of view for the film?

You can find the interview on our website:

Your First Fifteen Pages / Resources / Case Studies, worksheets, guides, and tips

The Hunger Games movie

Chapter 5: The Actions

"The writer's job is to get the main character up a tree, and then once they are up there, throw rocks at them."

—*Vladimir Nabokov*

We have a good friend who loves to talk. Whenever we get together, he tells us about everything happening in his life. His talk consists of lists – I went there, I saw this, I spoke to this person, I ate something, I left. He can go on like this for 30 minutes or more if no one breaks his chain of what: what he did, what he saw, what he ate, what he said. After each of these conversations, we walk away shaking our heads wondering why he thought it was important to convey that information to us. The *what* of his talk never seems to connect to a *why*.

Many of the submissions we read are like that. The writer piles detail after detail into the story, but when added together the details never seem to connect to the *why* of the story.

> *The actions your characters take, the dialogue they speak, the places you have them go and the things you have them do should all tie back to the inciting incident – the why of your story – or move toward the resolution.*

Let's dissect that statement. The point of the action in a novel is to move us from the inciting incident to the middle build of the novel and then on to the resolution. So, if you have action or dialogue in your novel that doesn't tie directly to either the inciting incident or is building toward the resolution, it needs to go. In *The Firm,* Grisham didn't write scenes showing Mitch interviewing with other firms. Why? Because the inciting incident was Mitch taking a job with a specific firm, even after Abby points out the job seems too good to be true. Yes, he dropped in a few hints about how sought-after Mitch was, but showing us more interviews wouldn't have supported the inciting incident or the resolution.

In *The Husband's Secret*, Cecilia finds the letter that changes her life when she goes to the attic to look for a piece of the Berlin Wall. At first, I thought the bit about the Berlin Wall was unrelated to the story until I realized that it serves two purposes. Looking for the piece of the Berlin Wall for her daughter gave Cecilia a reason to go to the attic and knock over the box where she found the letter. And it shows us how something so simple has the power to upend our lives.

Let's look at the chain of actions required to create the inciting incident in *The Husband's Secret*. Cecilia and her daughter Esther are talking about the Berlin Wall at breakfast. Cecilia remembers she has a piece of the wall and asks Esther if she'd like to have it. Always one to keep her promise, Cecilia goes to the attic to look for the piece of the wall and while she's looking, she knocks over a box with old tax documents in it. While she's putting the documents in the box, she comes across the letter. Cecilia's story and the book begins:

> *"It was all because of the Berlin Wall. If it weren't for the Berlin Wall, Cecilia would have never found the letter . . ."*

There were numerous other ways Cecilia could have discovered the letter but setting the letter up as old, forgotten, and mysterious and finding it in the attic in a box of stored tax papers works well.

Going to the attic to look for something is routine. Going to the attic to look for a piece of the Berlin Wall and finding a letter sets up a complication – to open or not to open the letter?

Actions create complications that drive the story forward. Complications in the first fifteen pages should all tie directly back to your inciting incident. Once we have an inciting incident, the complication *furthers* the action by creating a decision point or posing a dilemma that our protagonist must make or address by the end of the first chapter. In Cecilia's case, it was whether or not to tell John Paul she'd found the letter.

ACTION Cecilia tells Esther she has a piece of the Berlin wall, promises to find it.

ACTION Cecilia goes to the attic to keep her promise.

ACTION Cecilia knocks over boxes during her search.

INCITING INCIDENT She finds the letter.

ACTION After much internal debate she tells John Paul she found the letter.

COMPLICATION John Paul's reaction.

Action creates complications

In *The Hunger Games,* the inciting incident is Prim's name being called when there was only one chance of her being selected. After Prim's name is called Katniss is forced to make a decision – allow her sister to go to the Hunger Games or volunteer to go in her stead.

In *The Firm,* Mitch is offered a dream job that seems too good to be true. The inciting incident is the subtle warning from his wife Abby that something doesn't seem quite right. The dilemma is whether Mitch will heed Abby's warning or take the job.

In *The Invention of Wings,* the inciting incident is that Sarah is presented with her first slave, Handful. The dilemma is that Sarah must decide if she will follow the traditions and expectations of her family or refuse a "gift" when in her heart she feels slavery is morally wrong.

By the end of your first chapter or your first fifteen pages, we the reader need to know what the inciting incident is and we need to see the actions building from your inciting incident toward the complications, dilemmas, and decisions that begin to move your story forward.

BUILDING STORY THROUGH ACTION

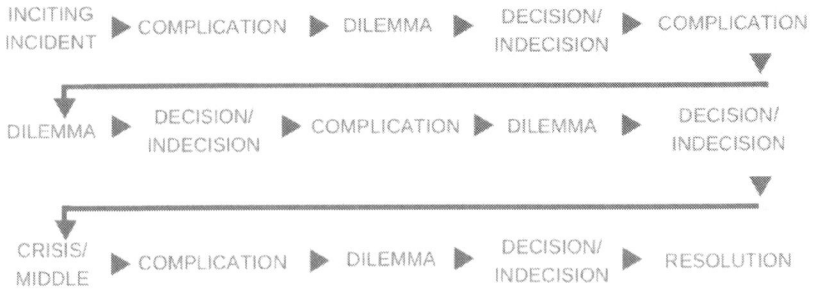

INCITING INCIDENT ▶ COMPLICATION ▶ DILEMMA ▶ DECISION/ INDECISION ▶ COMPLICATION

▼

DILEMMA ▶ DECISION/ INDECISION ▶ COMPLICATION ▶ DILEMMA ▶ DECISION/ INDECISION

▼

CRISIS/ MIDDLE ▶ COMPLICATION ▶ DILEMMA ▶ DECISION/ INDECISION ▶ RESOLUTION

Now that you understand the importance of revealing the inciting incident in your first fifteen pages, it's just as important not to let your story fall flat and waste the opportunity to continue building it through complications, dilemmas, and decisions/indecision that lead the reader to the crisis of the novel and the resolution. Let's explore what this looks like in more detail.

Throughout our lives, we are met with complications that pose a dilemma and require us to make a decision or waffle until our indecision creates another complication. For example, we find out a spouse has been cheating – INCITING INCIDENT which leads to a COMPLICATION in our relationship that poses a DILEMMA – to stay and try to work things out or leave – which ultimately leads to a DECISION. Let's say the decision is to leave. That decision leads to another COMPLICATION – where will I go? This creates a new DILEMMA – finding a place to live – requiring another DECISION. My new place is next door to the perfect guy but there is a COMPLICATION, he is in a relationship with my boss, who told me about my new apartment. DILEMMA – do I pursue the relationship? Or do I move again because I know he is the right one for me, but I respect my boss, even though she isn't in love with him? I decide to wait things out which is really INDECISION or inaction. Then, major CRISIS, my boss finds out she's pregnant, but in a twist, she confides it isn't my neighbor's baby. DILEMMA! Do I tell the potential love of my life she's pregnant with another man's baby OR do I keep her confidence, and possibly ruin his life and maybe ultimately mine? DECISION, I decide to keep my mouth shut and look for a new place to live. Then, just as I'm about to move, my boss announces she is leaving and moving to London to be with her true love, the father of the baby. RESOLUTION, I get the guy and a swanky new job to boot.

If I had written a story about a young woman who finds out her spouse is cheating, moves into a new apartment, meets a new guy, her boss gets pregnant and leaves, then she gets the guy and a great new job – We might have responded, "Whatever, yea for her." But when we layer on complications, dilemmas, and decisions/indecisions that build toward an ultimate crisis resulting in a test of character, faith, determination, or will for the main character, then a satisfying resolution – we have a much better story. By layering our story with complications, dilemmas, and decisions or indecisions, the reader will respond with, "I need to know more!" ending in a …"YEA!! What a great story!!!"

Developing a Character Through Action

> *Life always waits for some crisis to occur before revealing itself at its most brilliant.*
>
> *—Paulo Coelho*

Actions and dialogue shape the complications, dilemmas, and the decisions and indecisions of the characters. And each action or bit of dialogue should always harken back to the inciting incident and what is at stake for each character. For example, there is never a point in *The Invention of Wings* where the complications and dilemmas Sarah faces or the decision she makes aren't related to her struggle with the issue of slavery. Indeed, after leaving home, and giving up her position in society to gain the freedom to choose for herself, Sarah must ultimately choose between love, security, and her cause. Throughout the novel, Kidd stays focused on Sarah's struggle between freedom and enslavement that began with the gift of Handful when she was eleven.

In *The Firm*, Mitch is the poor kid striving to make it to the good life, who ignores his inner Cassandra and refuses to heed all the warning signs that the job with the firm might be too good to be true. The complications build from his refusal to see things for what they are until he must face facts and find a way out of the morass he has created.

The complication|dilemma|decision/indecision model for storytelling has been the go-to for the film industry since its inception. For some of you, it might be easier to see the progress of action that moves from a complication to a dilemma to a decision/or indecision, and then on to the next complication by looking at a film. And once we learn to recognize the progression in film, it is much easier to see it in books.

We'll use the movie version of *The Firm*, although distinctly different and much simpler than the novel, to illustrate the progression model.

INCITING INCIDENT Mitch is offered a job with a firm in Memphis. The offer is substantially more than he would make at other firms. When he tells Abby about the firm's offer, she hesitates and asks "Why?"

The firm flies Mitch and Abby to Memphis where they are wined and dined. COMPLICATION During their stay, Abby has an odd encounter with Kay, the wife of one of the firm's young attorneys. Kay tells Abby that, "Working isn't forbidden and the firm encourages children." DILEMMA Will Mitch heed Abby's second warning? DECISION After first telling her she's right. Mitch brushes off the warning and tells Abby everything will be fine. For a time, Mitch and Abby seem happily ensconced in their new life in Memphis. There are minor complications. The director shows Mitch staying late at the office night after night studying for the bar exam while Abby eats dinner alone. The stress is taking its toll, but this is the first year at a new firm and nothing they can't weather.

COMPLICATION Mitch and Abby arrive at the home of Kay and Lamar Quinn for dinner. Rather than the happy couple they were expecting, they find a grieving, tearful Kay and a despondent Lamar. Kay tells them two members of the firm, Marty Kozinski and Joe Hodges, were killed earlier that day in a boating accident while diving in the Cayman Islands. DILEMMA Mitch and Abby aren't' quite sure how to respond. They are new to the firm. They didn't know the people killed and the news was sad but doesn't seem to affect them directly. Abby confides to Mitch that Kay seemed more "scared" than upset.

DECISION Once again, Mitch ignores Abby's concerns then makes a joke to change the subject.

COMPLICATION Late one night, Mitch takes a break and goes to a diner for coffee. Two men come in and strike up a conversation. At some point in the conversation, they reference Marty Kozinski, Joe Hodges, Bob Lamm, and Allison Krauss, saying, "that's four dead lawyers out of 41 in less than ten years." DILEMMA What should Mitch do about the information dumped on him by two mysterious guys? DECISION He ponders the portraits of the dead attorneys back in the office but stays silent about the encounter.

The next scene offers another minor complication that sets up a much larger complication. Mitch and Abby fight about his coming home late once again. When Mitch tells her he is working hard for her, Abby counters telling him that it's not true and his need to achieve is about "a mother in a trailer park and a brother you pretend you don't have." *We'll talk more about that information in a few chapters.*

COMPLICATION The next day Mitch flies to the Cayman Islands with Avery Tolar, a senior partner who has taken Mitch under his wing. In a meeting with Sonny Capps, a major client, Sonny accuses Tolar of "making veiled threats" saying, "if you're talking about our friends in Chicago, they don't make money when I pay fees, you do. They make money being in business with me." DILEMMA Mitch has a difficult time ignoring Sonny's remarks and asks Avery about them after the meeting. Avery brushes Mitch's concerns off telling him, "We'll get into all of that." DECISION Mitch seeks out the owner of the dive company who chartered the boat to Hodges and Kozinski.

COMPLICATION Mitch returns to the condo just as Avery is getting ready for dinner. Avery tells him to get a beer and where the key is that opens the snack cabinet. Instead, Mitch mistakenly opens a closet where he finds file boxes labeled with the names of the dead lawyers. After a quick inspection of the files, he spills his beer and locks the cabinet. DILEMMA He has to hide what he's discovered from Avery. He deflects when Avery asks him where his beer is. DECISION Mitch keeps quite about what he's found.

COMPLICATION The firm sets Mitch up on the beach. After he saves a woman from an altercation with a man, she seduces him. DILEMMA Mitch, is faced with a choice, stay true to Abby or have sex with the woman on the beach? DECISION Mitch has sex with the woman and inadvertently provides the firm with something to use against him.

COMPLICATION Mitch decides he needs help and goes to see his brother Ray who is in prison a few hours away. DILEMMA After hearing everything Mitch has to say, Ray agrees Mitch is in way over his head. DECISION Ray puts Mitch in touch with Eddie Lomax, an ex-cop and private investigator in Little Rock, who did time with Ray.

Notice, up until the point where Mitch goes to see the owner of the boat charter company, *every action* Mitch takes ties back to the inciting incident. Mitch ignores all the warning signs. The over-inflated offer, the odd comments Kay makes to Abby about it not being "forbidden" for wives to work and that children encourage stability, and the couple's strange reaction to Hodges and Kocinski's deaths. He even brushes off the encounter with the men at the diner, until the comment by Sonny Caps alluding to mob connections finally pushes him to act.

Once he makes the turn toward action and away from blissful ignorance, all the action builds toward the crisis of the film, the point at which Mitch realizes that he has lost Abby. From that point on the action builds toward the resolution, how Mitch will keep his law license, free Ray, and win back Abby. We won't go through the rest of the complications, dilemmas, decisions, and indecision that create the remainder of the script because I want to stay focused on the first fifteen pages of your manuscript and how the cycle of complications, dilemmas, and decisions/indecisions moves your story and more importantly your reader along. By laying out the first quarter of the film *The Firm*, I wanted you to see how character drives the action. And, how the complications that arise in your story and the dilemmas your characters face should all tie back to the inciting incident *until* they move in the direction of the crisis, and then ultimately to the resolution. If you are interested in seeing if this model holds up, I encourage you to watch the film and see if you can pick the remaining sequences out for yourself.

I put a breakdown of the complications, dilemmas, decisions, and indecisions for *The Firm* up on the *Your First Fifteen Pages* website under Resources.

When the Action Doesn't Follow a Why

Recently, I opened a submission, and although the writing was lovely and the characters more distinguished than most, I finally decided to pass on the manuscript. Why? Because the actions – the complications, dilemmas, and decisions and indecision – over the course of the first fifteen pages didn't create enough interest or tension to make me ask for more.

Those first fifteen pages were missing an inciting incident, and because there wasn't an inciting incident, there wasn't a reason to act. It felt as if the writer had put people on stage and had them doing things – having conversations, writing in a journal, teasing one another, giving life advice – for no reason other than they had nothing else to do. Without an inciting incident, the actions had nothing to anchor them. No reason for happening. And without an inciting incident, the characters did not face any of the complications, dilemmas, or decisions that create tension and move a novel forward. So, I passed.

No matter how interesting a character might be, we don't read books with people walking around and saying things to one another for no reason. There has to be a point to the story, a driving factor, something that compels a character to act in a particular way.

Honestly, if we want to watch people go through their day without having anything at stake, we can go to work or dinner at mom's house. We don't need to pick up a book to understand tedium or everydayness. We pick up a book to be challenged by an idea, a dilemma, a fear, or a struggle. We pick up a book because we have a curiosity about *how* the characters in a story will overcome adversity, evil, loss, abandonment, heartbreak, or any of the myriad of other themes writers take on. We are curious because we all wonder what we would do if faced with a similar situation. And we want to learn something about a situation we have never experienced or would never put ourselves in.

Give readers a compelling inciting incident, a compounding complication, intriguing characters involved in things that relate directly to the inciting incident or the ultimate resolution, and they will follow your story from page to page. Leave them hanging on any of these, and they will close the book or turn off their Kindle before they get to page 20.

Actions Speak Louder Than Words

We've all heard this adage, but is it true of fiction? Again, let's look at how this applies to *The Hunger Games. In her first fifteen pages,* Suzanne Collins relies more on action than dialogue to develop the character of Katniss. What Katniss does, her actions, all build toward the inciting incident of Prim's name being chosen. Her actions in those first fifteen pages set up Katniss' decision to volunteer to take her sister's place at the beginning of the next chapter. Through her actions, we see *who* Katniss is and *why* she's made certain decisions. Let's walk through the important and building actions of the first fifteen pages of *The Hunger Games.*

The first thing Katniss does, in the first paragraph of the book, is reach for her little sister. That action is followed by information – "today is the day of the reaping." We might not know what the reaping is, but the word itself is ominous. From the beginning, we see Katniss as her sister's protector.

In the third paragraph, we learn that Katniss "tried to drown" Prim's cat "in a bucket" after she brought him home. While this action seems jarringly harsh for a young girl, Collins uses Katniss' internal dialogue to explain why "The last thing I needed was another mouth to feed." She relented because, "Prim begged so hard, cried even, I had to let him stay." COMPLICATION – She can't have another mouth to feed. DILEMMA – Prim begs her not to drown the cat. DECISION – Because she loves her sister, she allows her to keep the cat.

Four actions – reaching for her sister, attempting to drown a cat, Prim begging her not to, Katniss letting the cat live – build an image of two sisters, create tension, and move the story forward.

A few sentences later, we learn Katniss can "clean a kill" and 'see' her sliding into "hunting boots" grabbing for her forage bag." These actions show us someone determined to live, even if she has to eat a mouse or forage for food to do it.

We *see* Katniss crawling under fences and retrieving her bow and arrow, actions that further develop her character *and* work directly toward her decision to volunteer for Prim. Katniss tells us, through internal dialogue, that her actions are illegal and carry "the severest of penalties" that most people don't take the risk. Through her actions, Collins clearly *shows* us that Katniss is willing to do whatever it takes to feed her family, even risk jail.

Your First **15**

What your characters do, the actions they take, how they respond to the complications in your story and the complications themselves should be used to build the characters in your story and in turn move the tension and forward motion of the story itself.

For a new story, consider plotting:

1. The complications that will define your character, create tension, and move the story forward from the inciting incident to your crisis (the middle of your story).

2. Determine which character is at the heart of the complications. Use those complication to show us that main character.

For an existing story, identity:

1. If you have any complications built into your first fifteen pages and/or the pages leading up to your crisis.

2. If the complications in your first fifteen pages lead to clearly defined dilemmas and decisions or indecisions? If not, fill those in.

3. If not, map the complications you need to drive the story forward and define your main character.

Resources

1. Download the BUILDING YOUR STORY Airtable template from the website and use it to map the inciting incident, complications, dilemmas, decisions and indecision for your first fifteen pages and your book as you write.

2. Download *The Firm* – template example for Airtable.

Chapter 6: Dialogue

Without expressive dialogue, events lack depth, characters lose dimension, and story flattens.

—*Robert McKee*

Dialogue is not just quotation. It is grimaces, pauses, adjustments of blouse buttons, doodles on a napkin, and crossings of legs.

— *Jerome Stern*

Dialogue serves three functions in a story. First, dialogue can help build a character, especially if that character is significantly distinct. Second, the body language that accompanies dialogue gives us insight into the internal and external experience of a character. Third, you can use dialogue to introduce the inciting incident, move the action forward, and impart information, which we will cover in the next chapter.

The purpose of this chapter is not to teach you how to write great dialogue. There are excellent books for writing dialogue, which I list in the resources at the end of this chapter. The purpose of the chapter *is* to show you how to use dialogue in the first fifteen pages of your manuscript to introduce your inciting incident, move the action forward, and develop characters.

Building a Character Through Internal Dialogue

In *The Invention of Wings,* Sue Monk Kidd uses internal dialogue in the first few pages to show us how Handful views herself. Handful's thoughts are introspective and honest. Her view on life is resigned but a bit playful. She tells the reader,

> *"I was full of sass to Aunt-Sister about the whole miserable business. I'd say, 'Let this cup pass from me,' spouting one of missus' verses. I'd say, 'Jesus wept cause he's trapped in there with missus, like us.'"*

Handful is a house slave, who could read and write. Her internal dialogue is slightly more elevated than the language she uses around the "missus" or with the other slaves.

Sarah's life is the opposite of Handful's. She is educated and has access to her father's library and older siblings. She's grown up with privilege and freedom. Her talk is that of refinement and education. When we first meet Sarah, she is reflecting on the changes taking place in her life,

> *"My eleventh birthday began with Mother promoting me from the nursery. For a year I'd longed to escape the porcelain dolls, tops, and tiny tea sets strewn across the floor, the small beds lined up in a row, the whole glut and bedlam of the place, but now that the day had come, I balked at the threshold of my new room."*

Kidd does a masterful job of using internal dialogue to establish two very distinct characters that are held captive by their circumstances. Internal dialogue allows us to get to know Handful and Sarah. By the end of those crucial first fifteen pages, we've developed a relationship with them and want to know more about their lives.

Kidd also uses Sarah's internal dialogue to inform us about her relationship with her mother. Sarah is in her new room, adjusting to her new surroundings when her mother appears and asks her if her "new quarters were to my liking." Sarah's mother seems to bring out fear in her. She recalls that

> *"The door slammed in my throat, and the silence hung there. Mother looked at me and sighed. When she left, I willed my eyes to remain dry and turned away from Binah. I couldn't bear to hear one more Poor Miss Sarah."*

That bit of internal dialogue is needed to understand the inciting incident of the story, which comes on page 14. Sarah's mother ties a ribbon around Handful's neck and presents her to her daughter for her birthday. Kidd tells us that fear could not stop the words, Sarah:

> *"Pulled up from her throat like she was raising water from a well. When she finally got the bucket up, we could hardly hear what she was saying, '. . . . . I'm sorry, Mother . . . . . I can't accept." Missus asked her to say it over. This time Miss Sarah bellowed it like a shrimp peddler."*

The chapter ends on page 15 with Handful's mother issuing an ominous warning, "It gon be hard from here on, Handful."

The dialogue for Handful's mother is a bit rougher, less polished than her daughter. Her mother is a cautious, industrious woman and less educated than her daughter. Kidd shows this by infusing slightly more dialect into Mauma's talk and by using idioms such as, "bug be in the wheat 'fore long." But it is important to note that Kidd doesn't push the dialect to its breaking point. She doesn't use dialogue or language in a stereotypical way. Rather she emphasizes a few words here and there, just enough to show us that Mauma's talk is slightly different from her daughter's. For Mauma, gone is gon and before is 'fore. When we see those slight alterations in the text, our mind hears it as we read. Those tiny differences are enough to give us a sense of who Mauma is and how she sounds.

In addition, Kidd relies on sparse dialogue and sharp actions to draw the image of Sarah's mother. As Sarah is speaking her refusal, Handful tells us that Missus' "fingernails bore into me and carved out what looked like a flock of birds on my arm. She said, 'Sit down, Sarah dear.'"

Sarah's mother represents everything Sarah wants to escape. Her mother is the source of Sarah's complications and the resulting dilemmas, decisions, and indecisions she faces. Early in the first fifteen pages, Sarah becomes aware of the horrors of slavery. The inciting incident is her mother giving her a slave as a birthday present, setting up a complication for one so young. The dilemma for Sarah is whether she should accept the gift and follow the traditions of her family and culture quietly, accept the gift and reject it later, or reject the gift and risk her mother's wrath. When she bravely decides to reject her mother's gift of another human being she sets in motion all the complications that follow.

Without the use of internal dialogue in the pages that lead up to the inciting incident, we wouldn't understand what is at stake for Handful and Sarah, and we wouldn't feel as connected to them. By letting us into their thoughts, Kidd invites us to get to know her characters and encourages us to care for them.

Collins uses this same technique in *The Hunger Games*. The use of first person allows Katniss to tell us her story through internal dialogue, showing us what she sees and explaining what we need to know to understand what comes next. Without the use of internal dialogue, it would take much longer to build the world Katniss inhabits and much longer to get to the point of the story—Katniss' drive to protect her family and mainly her little sister. Around the bottom of page 15, Collins sets up the inciting incident with internal dialogue, "I protect Prim in every way I can, but I'm powerless against the reaping." The reaping is the complication. Every other day of the year, Katniss can and does protect Prim, but on the day of the reaping, she is powerless. Collins shows us Katniss' reaction to this loss of power, with the internal dialogue, "The anguish I feel when she's in pain wells up in my chest and threatens to register on my face."

Using internal dialogue, we see Katniss as a fierce and loving protector. And by the time Prim is chosen in the reaping, we ache for and with her.

Building a Character Through External Dialogue

Rowling uses external dialogue in the first fifteen pages of *Harry Potter and the Sorcerer's Stone* to give us clues to her characters. Consider this exchange between Professor McGonagall and Dumbledore:

> "A fine thing it would be if, on the very day You-Know-Who seems to have disappeared at last, if the Muggles found out about us all. I suppose he really has gone, Dumbledore?"

> *"It certainly seems so," said Dumbledore. "We have much to be thankful for. Would you care for a lemon drop?"*
>
> *"A what?"*
>
> *"A lemon drop. They are a kind of Muggle sweet I'm rather fond of."*
>
> *"No thank you," said Professor McGonagall coldly, as though she didn't think this was the moment for lemon drops.*

We learn a good bit about the characters from this simple exchange. We see that Professor McGonagall is always referred to by her title *professor,* while Dumbledore prefers a less formal greeting over Head Master or Professor Dumbledore. We see that in spite of the circumstances, Dumbledore is thankful and appreciative of the small things in life, like a lemon drop. Dumbledore appears a bit playful, offering a sweet treat to lighten the mood. Rowling uses this playful aspect of Dumbledore's personality as an endearing quirk throughout the series.

It is only after Professor McGonagall uses the moniker You-Know-Who for the second time, a few paragraphs later that Dumbledore gets a bit firm.

> *"My dear Professor, surely a sensible person like yourself can call him by his name? All this 'You-Know-Who' nonsense — for eleven years I've been trying to persuade people to call him by his name: Voldemort."*
>
> *Professor McGonagall flinched, but Dumbledore, who was unsticking two lemon drops seemed not to notice.*

In this exchange, Dumbledore refers to Professor McGonagall as sensible. And while he admonishes her for giving into the fear of Voldemort's name, he does it gently, using the lemon drops as a way of deflecting her discomfort. We see here a gentle, kind, and firm man. Rowling doesn't tell us Dumbledore was a gentle, kind, and firm man, rather she shows us these attributes through dialogue, while at the same time imparting important information to the reader.

In *The Husband's Secret*, there is a lovely exchange between Cecilia and her daughter that sets the tone of their relationship in the book:

> *"Esther," she called out again.*
>
> *"What is it?" Esther called back, in a patient, put-upon voice that Cecilia suspected was an unconscious imitation of her own.*
>
> *"Whose idea was it to build the Berlin Wall?"*
>
> *"Well, they're pretty sure it was Nikita Khrushchev's!" Esther answered immediately, pronouncing the exotic sounding name with great relish and her own peculiar interpretation of a Russian accent.*
>
> *"He was like, the prime minister of Russia, except he was the premier."*

From this bit of dialogue, we see that Cecilia views her daughter as a trusted source. And, we see Esther as a smart, confident person her mother turns to for information, even though she is quite young.

Simply by adding small character hints into the dialogue such as "patient" and "put upon voice," we see Esther more clearly.

Using Dialogue to Show a Character's Experience

Shortly after the scene where Sarah rejects her gift, Handful, frightened by the circumstances swirling around her, wets herself in front of Misses' guests. Back in their cabin, her mother attempts to comfort her, telling her that "Everything gon be alright." But for Handful, "the shame stayed with me. I tasted it like a bitter green on my tongue."

Rather than telling the reader Handful felt ashamed, Kidd uses an analogy Handful might use and that we could understand—shame tasted like a bitter green.

Kidd also shows us Sarah's experience through dialogue. After seeing a family slave whipped, Sarah runs away. When she returns home, her mother shakes her and demands she promise that she will never run away again. Sarah responds internally telling us:

"I want to. I try to. The words are on my tongue–the round lumps of them, shining like marbles.

"Sarah!" she demands.

"Nothing comes out. Not a sound."

Her mother's ferocity renders Sarah mute. This interaction sets up the relationship between Sarah and her mother and builds to the point in the novel where Sarah literally finds her voice. Kidd knows that for her reader to understand the growth Sarah goes through as a woman, it is imperative to understand that the muteness she experienced as a child began when she encountered the horrors of slavery.

Developing an Ear for Dialogue

One of the best ways to develop an ear for dialogue is to listen to people talk. Sit in a coffee shop and listen to the talk around you. Sit back at family gatherings and listen to the banter between siblings and cousins. When you get your next haircut, eavesdrop on the conversation between the stylist and client in the next chair. Hang around the water cooler.

If you set your book in another period, watch movies from that period. Steal like an artist (thank you Austin Kleon). Actors and directors bring in dialect coaches, historians, and experts to ensure they are getting the period right. Use what came before as a classroom to inform your writing.

Read books from the actual period, not books *about* the period, those by authors who wrote during your specific period. Don't simply assume that everyone in the seventeen century was using the same stilted, formal language regardless of class. Then, as now, speech reflected class, education, gender, and a myriad of other information you can use to capture the period.

Be open to suggestion, but be wary of those who are unfamiliar with the characters or the dialect in your story. When I was in graduate school, I took a creative writing course with a marginally published author. Everyone in the class except me dressed in all black, wore Doc Martins, and were deeply into minimalism. Think Hemingway meets the angst of the antiwar movement and the very, very early days of the coming out movement. The prose they produced was spare, flat, and emotionless.

I wore color. I wrote in long endless sentences full of emotion. My stories relied on complicated characters that fell in love with the wrong people, ruined their lives and the lives of those around them, and learned from their choices. Because I was from the South, some of my characters spoke with a Southern dialect. After reading aloud one day, one of my classmates looked and me and with total earnestness said, "No one talks that way anymore." Uh, no one except the 100 plus million people living in *the South*.

The students in that class were mainly from Salt Lake City, which was a very homogenous place to grow up, where accents were nonexistent. Their talk was polite and very correct with little emotional inflection. Minimalism was a perfect choice for these writers. For a girl from the South, it was nearly impossible to mimic with any accuracy, until I spent a year or two listening to the unaccented, mildly upbeat newscaster dialect that my students and classmates spoke. But I still wrote mainly about what I knew – the class, race, and gendered nuisances of Southern life and relationships.

Choose the words and dialect for your characters that are authentic to who they are, what they are doing, and the period. If you aren't sure, find someone who does what your character does or lives as your character lives. Volunteer at a school to hear how children a certain age speak or babysit your sister's kids for the weekend. If you aren't sure how nurses interact, but you have a scene in a hospital, go hang out at a nurse's station. If you need to understand how police talk, sign up to go on a ride-along. Many local police departments offer classes and ride-alongs as part of their citizens' academy programs. If you have an important character that is outside your wheelhouse, find films to watch featuring a similar character.

Getting the dialogue right will go a long way toward helping your reader develop a strong relationship with your characters.

Using Dialogue to Introduce the Inciting Incident or Move Action Forward

Often, we read submissions heavy with dialogue that seem to serve no purpose other than having the characters in the story talking to one another. The dialogue isn't there to define the characters or remark on the setting. Rather, the characters are engaged in what communications scholars refer to as phatic communication. The writer has everyone in the story chatting about the weather or how slow a train is or how well they did or didn't sleep. Small talk, the niceties we engage in every day, doesn't belong in novels. And filling your first fifteen pages full of meaningless conversation is a sure way to kill the chance of having anything read past page 15.

Here's an example from a submission we recently received:

> *"Are you okay?"*
>
> *"I think so," she said and shrugged, hesitating at the door hoping her body language would convey what she was thinking.*
>
> *He started to unlock the car and stopped.*
>
> *"Are you sure you're okay?" he asked her again. His words partially snatched by a gust of wind.*
>
> *"Yes," she said, quietly.*

This bit of dialogue comes after a couple of dense paragraphs about isolation that attempts to situate the reader in place and build tension, but because the writer withheld everything from the reader, I had no idea what was going on or who the characters were. And without an inciting incident to ground the reading, I had no idea what the story was about or why I was reading it.

Now let's look at dialogue written to move the action forward. After revealing that Voldemort has killed the Potters, Rowling continues the conversation between Professor McGonagall and Dumbledore:

> *Professor McGonagall's voice trembled as she went on. 'That's not all. They're saying that he tried to kill the Potter's son Harry. But – he couldn't. He couldn't kill that little boy. No one knows*

why, or how, but they're saying when he couldn't kill Harry Potter, Voldemort's powers somehow broke – and that's why he's gone."

Dumbledore nodded glumly.

"It's – it's true?" Professor McGonagall faltered. "After all he's done . . . after all the people he's killed . . . he couldn't kill a little boy?"

And now, we are wondering how the boy was able to withstand the evil Voldemort? And how did he survive?

There were other ways that Rowling could have introduced the inciting incident, Harry's survival, his being orphaned, and coming to live with the Dursleys. She could have shown us the battle itself and the way Harry's mother fought to save him. But the battle and Voldemort are not at the beginning of the novel, because they are not the true focus. At the beginning of the novel and the series itself, the true focus is Harry. For Harry to discover that he comes from a wizarding family and that he has been accepted to Hogwarts. The beginning of Harry's long battle with Voldemort doesn't come until the final chapter when Professor Quirrel unveils Voldemort to the reader for the first time. Up to that point, Voldemort is a legend, not a reality.

By introducing Voldemort in this way and telling us Harry survived his attack, we understand that there is something special or significant about Harry. Rowling uses the rest of the novel to show us what that is. We learn that Harry comes from a wizarding family, that he has been accepted into a school for wizards, and that Harry is brave, because he makes the decision to protect the Sorcerer's Stone from Snape and Voldemort.

The dialogue in your story serves a purpose. When your characters speak, be sure they are saying something meaningful, not simply passing the time or wasting the reader's time or willingness to engage in your story. Dialogue is a powerful tool in the writing toolbox. Use it to introduce your inciting incident, develop complications and your characters, explain dilemmas, decisions, and indecisions and to move the action toward the climax and resolution of your story.

A Note on the F-Word

One of the first books we signed at RO was a book by Michelle Rene called *Hour Glass*. It is a lovely story about an unlikely and unexpected family set in the wild West. One of the main characters in the story is Calamity Jane. If you've read anything about Jane or watched "Deadwood," the HBO series about the town of Deadwood featuring Ian McShane, Timothy Oliphant, and Robin Weigert as Calamity Jane, you expect a certain level of profanity.

When we first signed the book, I tried to read it without the cussing, and primarily without the use of the word *fuck* by Jane. And frankly, the dialogue felt unauthentic and flat. Historians, authors, and directors have portrayed Jane as a tough woman who could drink, shoot, and cuss better than most of the men she encountered. To clean up her language to suit those readers who find the f-word bothersome, would have neutered the story and Jane.

I have a friend who loves using the f-word and every other cuss word ever invented. She writes like she speaks, peppering her writing with words intended to shock, surprise, and get a laugh. Her language, like Jane's, is part of who she is. The opposite end of the spectrum is my father, a retired Command Sergeant Major who spent 25 years in the service and rarely ever cusses. If I wrote a character based on my father and I filled his dialogue with expletives, I would be writing against type. If I wrote my friend without cussing, I would miss the essence of who she is.

I love a well-chosen cuss word or two, or even three if they make sense for the character and the situation. If they don't, there are plenty of other words to choose from.

Your First 15

For a new story, consider how to use dialogue:

1. Are there ways that you can introduce and complicate characters through dialogue?

2. Is dialogue the best or only way to introduce your inciting incident?

3. Can you use dialogue to develop complications or show us the dilemmas, decisions, indecisions your characters are facing?

For an existing story, identity:

1. If your dialogue is serving a purpose or do you simply have characters engaging in small talk?

2. If you have complications, dilemmas, decisions or indecisions that could be heightened through dialogue.

3. If all the dialogue in your story is linked to the inciting incident or a complication. If not, rewrite it.

Resources

1. *Robert McKee, Dialogue: The Art of Verbal Action for Page, Stage and Screen*

2. Any movie written by Nora Ephron. Ephron was the queen of dialogue. Her characters speak and think the way we all want to speak and act. The interactions feel real. You might not be a fan of romantic comedies but trust me, if your novel is about real people doing real things Ephron is your teacher. My favorites are:

   * *When Harry Met Sally*

   * *You've Got Mail*

- *Sleepless in Seattle*

- *Michael*

- *Julie & Julia*

3. Read. Get five of the best books in your genre and read for dialogue. Underline, highlight, or copy the dialogue into a journal. Take notes. How does the author use the dialogue? To define a character? To introduce the inciting incident? To move the action along? See how other writers use dialogue and learn from them.

Chapter 7: Imparting Information

Most people say, "Show, don't tell," but I stand by Show and Tell, because when writers put their work out into the world, they're like kids bringing their broken unicorns and chewed-up teddy bears into class in the sad hope that someone else will love them as much as they do.

—Colson Whitehead

There are times when you will need to convey information to fill in the gaps for the reader. There are a number of techniques for imparting information. Writers use *internal dialogue* or thoughts in a first person point of view. *Narration* can carry information in third person point of view, and *dialogue* works to convey information for both first and third person.

In *The Hunger Games,* Collins uses internal dialogue to fill the reader in on certain facts. Katniss tells the reader that normally the part of the "Seam" where she lives would be "crawling with coal miners heading out to the morning shift at this hour. Men and women with hunched shoulders, swollen knuckles, many who have long since stopped trying to scrub the coal dust out of their broken nails, the lines of their sunken faces."

Even though she is imparting information, the images are vivid. Our minds immediately conjure pictures of haunted looking coal miners emerging from a shaft with faces covered in grime.

When you need to bring your reader up to speed, make information part of the story, rather than pulling us out of the dialogue or action.

Too often writers impart information in a way that pulls the reader out of the story, and when the information has passed, forces them once again to settle back down into the story. Don't be that writer.

In the previous chapter, we covered how internal and external dialogue works. Let's spend a bit of time on how to use narration in the third person point of view.

Using Narration to Convey Information

Writers use narration to set up a scene, describe setting, signal a major change is coming, and to explain a character's actions. Like dialogue, narration should move the story along and tie directly to your inciting incident in the first fifteen pages or build toward your resolution. If you have long passages of narration that don't serve a specific purpose in the book, kill those darlings, because chances are they are bogging down your story.

The excerpt below is from a chick-lit novel I wrote years ago and keep around as a teaching tool. Near the beginning of the novel, there is a section of narration that goes on for pages.

> Every August, Shelby's family gathered at Trinity Oaks, her father-in-law's family home on Emerald Isle, off the coast of North Carolina, for what should be a fun, bonding time for four generations of Reynolds. But, given that Clayton Preston Reynolds has more money than God, it is heavy on the mandatory and light on the fun. Things got worse after Shelby and her husband Adam gave birth to Morgan, the first Clayton Preston Reynolds grandchild. Since then, Clayton has held the money over their heads, like a sprig of mistletoe at Christmas. Neither looks dangerous until you realize the person you have to suck up to might expect a lot more than you want to give.
>
> Morgan, now five, attends Latin Day where three generations of Reynolds have gone before her. Clayton pays for Latin Day and all of Morgan's other activities. All Shelby and Adam have to do is show up at seven or eight mandatory family events each year and pretend they are happy to be there.
>
> Hey, I would do it too, if my father-in-law had Clayton Preston Reynolds' money and was still alive. But alas, I am married to a poor orphaned academic with no lineage or family to speak of. Which means no big inheritance, but it sure makes decisions about how to spend holidays a whole lot easier.
>
> But August at the beach means missing out on gossip and the food and fun of Bunco back at home in Greensboro. More specifically, it is Friendship Cove, a quaint, eclectic neighborhood on the southern shore of Elm Lake.

Looking back, I now know that the information I was imparting was not all relevant to the inciting incident, which happens past page 15 and the bits of information that were important *should* have been conveyed through dialogue or with considerably more showing and much less telling.

Now, let's look at an example of how to impart information using narration that works. The opening paragraph of *The Firm* begins:

> *The senior partner studied the resume for the hundredth time and again found nothing he disliked about Mitchell Y. McDeere, at least not on paper. He had the brains, the ambition, the good looks. And he was hungry . . .*

This narration continues for four paragraphs. Throughout those paragraphs, Grisham drops hint-after-hint that all lead to the inciting incident. He indicates that being "hungry" was something the firm looked for. As was being married which was "mandatory." Later we realize that single people have less to lose than married people and especially those with children. A single person might be willing to risk his life to leave the firm, but someone with a wife and child probably won't. We learn that the firm specializes in taxes and Mitch is a CPA, as well as a soon to be lawyer. The firm is racist and sexist, having never hired a black person and only one woman, a "mistake" that ended in a car accident. We also see that as the partner reflects on the loss of a member of the firm, there is no sorrow reflected.

In the next paragraph, we learn that the firm had a report on Mitch compiled by "some ex-CIA agents in a private intelligence outfit in Bethesda." While today this might not seem odd, when *The Firm* was published in 1996, this revelation should have been a red flag to the reader. We also learn Mitch has a large student loan and Grisham repeats a second time, Mitch is "hungry."

This section of narration tells us a good bit of backstory about the firm and Mitch. We know why the firm is seeking Mitch out, they always go after the brightest student when they recruit what they feel will fit in their old boy culture. This particular year, Mitch is the prize. In the next scene, Mitch arrives for his interview and Grisham switches to dialogue.

Through dialogue, we learn about Mitch's family. His father was a coal miner and died in a mining accident. He played football in high school, which lead to a scholarship. His mother remarried and moved to Florida. No hint that they are close or that he sees her. He had two brothers. One killed in Vietnam, the other he refuses to discuss. We learn that he both reveres and adores his wife, Abby. And that he has done his homework and knows a good bit about the members of the firm.

Grisham layers more hints about the firm in the conversation. Oliver Lambert, a senior partner, tells Mitch that the members of the firm are "a close-knit fraternity" and that it is "extremely rare" for someone to leave. Mr. Knight echoes his words telling Mitch, that "the average turnover rate" for firms "our size or larger was twenty-eight percent." While at the firm, the turnover rate year after year has been "zero."

At the end of this scene, Grisham tells us again "They knew he seldom slept. They knew he was hungry. He was their man."

There is a lot of information packed in the narration and the dialogue of those first nine pages. Grisham is setting both the reader and Mitch up. We might have a slight inclination that something isn't quite right. Grisham doesn't come right out and tell us the firm is in bed with the mob, or that if he decides to leave Mitch will have to die and take his wife with him. Instead, Grisham drops hints, little clues that will pay off later in the story. And most importantly, everything in those first pages ties directly to the inciting incident, the fact that Mitch is indeed too hungry, too eager to shed the poverty of his childhood to pay attention to the subtle warning signs. It is Abby who on page 13 gives us the inciting incident when she says "I don't understand Mitch. Why are they being so generous?"

Abby serves as the Cassandra in Grisham's story. In Greek mythology, Cassandra was cursed to utter prophecies that were true, but no one heeded. Grisham uses Abby in this role numerous times in the novel.

In *The Husband's Secret,* Moriarty uses narration to tell us important information about Cecilia's husband, early in the story. We learn on page 11 that John-Paul can't go in the attic because he is terribly claustrophobic and "avoids taking the elevator." He also has "regular nightmares about being trapped in a room where the walls were contracting." This bit of narration hints that John-Paul has a secret so troubling, it haunts his dreams. These are not simply interesting character traits. There is a reason Moriarty focused on them, and as we learn more about John-Paul's secret, his claustrophobia and dreams make sense.

Describing Setting

When Cecilia goes to look for the piece of the Berlin wall, Moriarty knows she will knock over boxes in her search. If the attic were large and spacious, the kind of attic that spanned the entire house and could at some point become a room, the space would have to be filled to the brim with discarded furniture, boxes, maybe even Christmas decorations. But an attic that cluttered and disorganized would work against the character she's established in Cecilia.

The attic in Cecilia's home is more of a "storage area in the roof space. You reached it by pulling down a ladder from a trapdoor in the ceiling." We immediately picture a small cramped space, which the narrator tells us is nonetheless "tidy and well organized" because Cecilia would have it no other way. This gives Moriarty room to describe how Cecilia's organizing talent, made her a "minor celebrity." So of course, anything she stored in the attic was "stacked with clearly labeled white plastic containers." John-Paul, however, preferred to store their financial records, his domain, in "shoe boxes."

This description is so well written that we can *see* the space. We can see the plastic bins all neatly labeled and stacked. And we can see the precarious "tower of shoe boxes" Cecilia knocks over when she hears the phone ring, "startling her out of the past."

Think about your settings. Have you imparted a description of them that provides the clues we need to fill in the scene? Or have you included information about setting that doesn't support the inciting incident or other elements of your story? Have you told us the color of the sofa? What appears outside the window? And the temperature of a room that people are only passing through to get to the kitchen?

As readers, we need bits of information to ground us in your story. Sharing too little or over-sharing is a balancing act. As writers, we need to walk the rope and keep adding, or cutting until we get the balance exactly right.

Signaling a Story Shift

In *The Hunger Games,* after Katniss returns from the woods, she finds her mother and sister dressed and ready for the Reaping ceremony. She tells us, "a tub of warm water waits" for her. She cleans up and puts on a dress her mother has laid out for her. The dress is "one of her own lovely dresses." As Katniss prepares herself for the ceremony, we get the sense that something is about to change. That Katniss is moving toward something. That she is no longer a child, or at least that whatever trace of childhood that might remain, is about to be extinguished. She is preparing for her next role, that of tribute, even if she doesn't quite know it.

In *Harry Potter and the Sorcerer's Stone,* when Dumbledore "steps over the low garden wall," and lays Harry "gently on the doorstep" then tucks a letter inside the blankets, we know something is about to change. For both the Dursleys and for Harry Potter. This scene comes full circle when Dumbledore walks back down the street and clicks the "Putter-Outer" returning light to the lampposts.

We don't discover until much later in the series why Harry must return to the Dursleys year-after-year and why as a baby, Dumbledore placed him in the care of an aunt and uncle who detested him. We don't need to know that in book one. But we do need to know that Harry is an orphan, he has living relatives, and it is painful for Professor McGonagall, Dumbledore, and Hagrid to let him go. Rowling sticks to revealing the bits of information that are all important to book one in the series, and only book one.

Explaining a Character's Action

You may need to provide information either through dialogue or narration to explain a character's actions. In the second chapter of *The Inventions of Wings,* Sarah recalls the first time she witnessed the beating of a slave. Rosetta was old and as she was dragged from the barn and tied to the porch, Sarah's mother "watched impassively." Sarah hears the woman beg her mother, *"Missus please. Missus. Missus. Please."* She watches the blood bloom onto her yellow dress and is confused by the beauty of the roses that grow up the porch and the flowers of blood blossoming on the back of the slave as she's beaten. She recoils at the thought of her mother counting the lashes, *"Thirteen. Fourteen."* Finally, when she can no longer watch, Sarah bolts and runs away.

Without this scene, this information, we wouldn't understand Sarah's refusal of Handful a bit later in the story. We need to know that Sarah is not only repulsed by slavery, but by her mother's indifference to the brutality of the institution. By providing this scene early in Sarah's chapter, we come to view Sarah as different from her mother and from those who accept slavery as a part of life.

This scene also sets up the inciting incident to come. It explains why Sarah is willing to risk her mother's wrath by refusing the gift of Handful. It isn't just slavery she is rejecting. She is also telling her mother through the refusal that she will not be like her.

When a writer includes these layers of information for the reader, they are following their instincts. Sue Monk Kidd understood that we needed to understand Sarah's motivations, to understand why she went against her mother, her culture, and accepted tradition. Often information comes from asking why. Why did a young eleven-year-old girl stand up to her mother and refuse her gift? Because she'd witnessed the brutality of slavery first-hand, at the hands of her own mother.

Go through your first fifteen pages. Look for the whys of your story. Is there any place where we need more information to understand the setting, the motivations, or actions of a character or to move the story along?

Your First 15

Review the ways that you can convey information to your reader. Think about how you might use internal dialogue, narration, and external dialogue to provide the information your reader needs to understand where the story is going.

For a new story, consider where you might need to add information:

1. To explain a character's actions?

2. To signal a shift in the story?

3. To describe a setting?

4. To convey necessary information to the reader?

For an existing story, identity:

1. Long passages of narration that aren't serving the story.

2. Places where information would help move the story forward.

3. Areas of your story that lead to a why. Why is the character acting that way? Why this setting as opposed to another? Add any information needed to clear up the why.

4. How to signal a significant shift in your story through information. Hint: do this through showing not telling.

Resources

1. Pick one of the exemplars we are using throughout this book and highlight all of the places where information is used to move the story along.

2. Pick one or two of the ways the authors of our exemplars impart information and see if you can model it in your first fifteen pages.

Chapter 8: Setting

"Besides furnishing a plausible abode for the novel's world of feeling, place has a good deal to do with making the characters real, that is, themselves, and keeping them so."

—*Eudora Welty, On Writing*

The first fifteen pages of our exemplars take place in a hotel suite, a kitchen, a place called District 12, a plantation, and on a suburban street. Some of these settings require very little detail to conjure an image of place in the reader's mind. One required the writer to create a world for us using very specific language and details.

How intricate you make your setting depends on how familiar we are with the world your story inhabits. There are two ways to create the setting of your story. You can allow the reader to extrapolate the setting from his or her previous experience or you can draw the setting using thick description.

Subtly Inferring Setting

Rather than simply telling us that Mitch's interview was held in a large, expensive hotel suite, Grisham shows us using just enough detail to allow us to create the setting based on previous experience. I've highlighted his language choice in the excerpts below:

> *"Lamar* strolled nonchalantly across *the thousand-dollar-a-day suite and poured another cup of decaf. He checked his watch. He glanced at the two partners* sitting at the small conference table near the windows.*"

> *"They sat around a* shiny mahogany conference table *and exchanged pleasantries. McDeere* unbuttoned his coat and crossed his legs.*"*

> *"Why are we interviewing in a hotel room? The other firms interview on campus through the placement office."*

> *"Perhaps I can answer that Mitch," said Royce McKnight, the managing partner. "You must understand our firm. We are different, and we take pride in that . . . we keep a low profile, and we do things differently."*

You can see that Grisham doesn't spend a lot of time on drawing the setting for us. He uses setting to convey two things. First that the firm is wealthy and can afford to interview in an expansive suite and second, that the firm does things "differently" a statement that stirs our suspicions.

Grisham doesn't need to go overboard with his description of the hotel room. He only uses one tell, "thousand-dollar-a-day suite," the rest of his description of place is heavy on showing. We've seen expensive, expansive suites on TV or we've had the occasion to attend a meeting, perhaps even an interview in a suite ourselves. We generally know what one looks like, and from experience, we can fill in the blanks. But by having Lamar "stroll nonchalantly across" the suite, we immediately envision a suite spacious enough for strolling. This isn't a room at the Holiday Inn where strolling would be impossible. This is an expansive space, in an upscale, high-end hotel. The kind of hotel where guests are greeted by valets, thick plush carpets line the halls, and lush plants adorn the lobby. This is a suite with a mahogany conference table with room to cross your legs, rather than a small cramped pine table that requires you to tuck your legs tightly under for fear you will kick someone. With those few details, our minds create a mental picture of the hotel suite where the interview takes place.

The same is true of the opening scene in *The Husband's Secret*. Cecilia is "sitting here at the kitchen table." After a few minutes of contemplating the letter she "filled the kettle, switched it on, and cleaned the droplets of water in the sink with a paper towel till it shone." With just that reference, our minds flick away images of a messy, disorganized kitchen crawling with roaches, filling in the kitchen that our character Cecilia, an organized, super tidy person would live in.

Does it matter for the story what the cabinets look like? Or, if the countertop is granite or tile? Does it matter if the floors are slate or wood? No. All we need to know is that Cecilia is sitting in her kitchen staring at a letter, trying to decide whether or not to open it. Moriarty lets her reader fill in the details of the scene themselves because she knows we can.

Think about your opening scene. Is it set in a space that is easily conjured up in the reader's mind? A library, a bedroom, a car, on the beach? Have you given the reader two or three clues about your setting? Or have you loaded the reader with unnecessary details? A submission I read a few months back was burdened with details about the character's office. The writer described in painstaking detail what was on the floor, on the walls, on the desk, outside the window and then described the windows themselves telling the reader they were "tall arched windows with rippling glass that ever so slightly obscured Link's view of the world." Yowza! It was exhaustively overwritten and grueling to read. Just tell us Link's office was on the fourth floor of an ancient building and filled with books. We can fill in the rest.

World Building

The flipside of Grisham's scant setting is the more intricate *world building* Collins must do to place us within the world of Katniss. District 12 and the country of Panem don't exist. They, like Hogwarts in *Harry Potter*, were created in the imagination of their authors. For us to understand the desperate poverty Katniss and her family live with and the lack of freedom that permeates her life, Collins spends a good bit of time in the first fifteen pages showing us Katniss' world. And yet, she still allows the reader to fill in what she knows we can.

> *"Our part of District 12, nicknamed the Seam, is usually crawling with coal miners heading out the morning shift at this hour. . . But today the black cinder streets are empty. Shutters on the squat grey houses are closed."*

Katniss' world is dingy, grey, and covered in coal dust. Without this attention to detail, there would be no way for us to understand what motivates Katniss both to hunt and to protect her sister. But it isn't necessary for Collins to beat the picture into our heads. In just a few sentences using thick details, we see the Seam before us.

Later in the book, Collins must create the Capital and the arena for her reader. Here too, she offers enough description for us to visualize the Capital without spending pages describing the city to the reader.

There are many good examples of world building. The modern masters of this writing technique are J. R. R. Tolkien, C. S. Lewis, and George R. R. Martin. The list could go on and on. If you need to construct a world for your readers, I recommend reading novels by these and other authors you find who have come before you. Learn from the masters.

Using Setting to Infer Position and Relationship

In *Harry Potter and the Sorcerer's Stone,* Rowling uses setting in a deft way to signal difference. Most of the action around the Dursleys happens *inside*, while all of the action surrounding Professor McGonagall, Dumbledore, Hagrid, and Harry happens *outside*. She could have had the discussion between Dumbledore and Professor McGonagall take place at Hogwarts or any other number of places. But, by choosing to set the action *outside*, Rowling reinforces the idea that these are people outside the norm, different from the Dursleys in every possible way.

In the next chapter, Rowling also uses setting to distinguish how Harry is different than the rest of his family by having him live in a cupboard under the stairs. The location of Harry's room in the house sets the tone for his place in the family pecking order. By giving him a broom closet for a room, Rowling doesn't have to go into detail about how much the Dursleys dislike having Harry around. Even a ten-year-old reader can figure that out from the clues Rowling builds in around setting.

Using Language to Infer Setting

In *The Invention of Wings*, the author uses language to signal when we are in a different place and time. She begins the book with a description of Handful's day taking us through "boiling slave bedding, stoking the fire under the wash pot." We are clearly in a time before washing machines, before electricity, before the Civil War. She then orients the reader to the time of year telling us that the sun was "a little button stitched tight to the sky" and that she was wearing her sack, a "thickset coat made of heavy yarn," rather than the light dress she'd worn in the summer.

Kidd uses the references of the time-period, telling us that while Handful's given name is Hattie, her "basket name," the name her mauma gave her when she looked at her in the basket was Handful because "I was born too soon." With that brief bit of information, we are oriented to both time and place, pre-Civil War America and it is winter.

Your First 15

Think about the role place has in your story. Is your story set in a conventional setting that your reader will easily understand? Or, do you need to build an entire world for the reader?

For a new story, determine:

1. The place and time of your story.

2. If there are ways you can use place (inside/outside, upstairs/downstairs, corner office/cubical) to draw distinctions between groups or specific people in the story.

3. Ways to describe time, if it is important to your story, without telling us that your story is set in December or within a specific period.

For an existing story, identity:

1. If you have over described your setting.

2. If any of the suggestions for a new story above will improve your work.

3. Places you can infuse the senses into your first fifteen pages to create more layers in your writing and your story.

Resources

1. Go on a wander in nature. Listen for the sounds that surround you. Take a journal and record the sounds you hear. Back at your desk or in your favorite writing spot, add active verbs to describe your wander in more detail.

2. Either fix a meal or go to a restaurant to eat. Eat slowly, savoring each and every bite. Take a journal and describe the tastes your encounter. Describe the texture of the food, the color, the smells.

3. Go to a museum and sit in front of a painting. Describe what you see. Describe the colors, the textures, the light, the frame, the brush strokes. Add active verbs to your description.

4. Have a friend arrange a tray with ten items. Before seeing the items, put on a blindfold and no peeking. Using your phone, record your description of each item. What does it feel like? Is it rough, smooth, heavy, or light? Can you come up with a metaphor for what you are feeling? Does it feel like alligator skin or soft like the hair of a baby? Take the blindfold off and layer your description more now that you know what the objects are.

Chapter 9: Delicious Details

If you say in the first chapter that there is a rifle hanging on a wall, in the second or third chapter it absolutely must go off. If it's not going to be fired, it shouldn't be hanging there.

—S. Shchukin, Memoirs adapted from Valdimir Nabokov

Don't tell me the moon is shining, show me the glint of light on broken glass."

—Anton Chekov

Delicious details are the setups and payoffs, quirks and eccentricities, descriptions, unexpected twists, turns of phrase, and emotional investments that you work into your story. These details are the icing on your cake that often comes after the first or second or even third draft. They are the juicy bits of writing that, if done well, stick with readers for weeks and occasionally years after they've closed your book.

Adding these details help create characters such as Hannibal Lector, Harry Potter, or the Bennett sisters that a reader remembers a decade later.

The details might take the form of a setting that lingers in our minds such as Hogwarts, or Padua, the house in *The Keeper of Lost Things,* or the arena in *The Hunger Games.*

It could create a quirky reference such as the "lovely cup of tea" from *The Keeper of Lost Things.* After reading the book, my husband and I began to refer to our morning cup as the lovely cup of coffee.

It could be a story concept so profound it defines a generation – *The Handmaid's Tale, One Flew Over the Cuckoo's Nest*, and *On the Road*.

When you combine words in just the right way, the details become a feast for your reader. The rest of the chapter discusses ways to infuse delicious details into your first fifteen pages and the rest of your novel.

Setup and Payoff

This technique involves dropping in a hint, or a reference to something (the setup), and then later in the chapter or book return to it in a significant way (the payoff). JK Rowling is a master of setup and payoff. Throughout the Harry Potter series, she drops in references to an ability or object and then returns to it later in the book or the series. She may introduce something like Harry's ability to understand snakes early on (setup) and then in another book, reveal that he can also speak to snakes (payoff). For example, in Book 1, *Harry Potter and the Sorcerer's Stone,* we learn Harry is different when he hears a snake at the zoo. In Book 2, *The Chamber of Secrets,* Harry learns he can talk to snakes, and he is a Parselmouth. In Book 4, we discover Voldemort is also a Parselmouth. What seems like a small complication and dilemma in Book 1 – Harry encountering the snake and confirming he is different – becomes a major plot twist in Books 2 and 4. It is only when we look at it after finishing the series that we realize how effectively Rowling used setup and payoff.

Using setup and payoff well creates a full circle story. Near the beginning of *The Keeper of Lost Things,* after Anthony's fiancé is killed (inciting incident) Anthony loses the medal that his fiancé gave him (complication). The medal returns to Anthony near the end of the novel (resolution) in a beautiful and unexpected way. I won't spoil the story for you. You'll have to read it to see how Ruth Hogan works this bit of setup and payoff magic.

Setup and payoff can be used to bracket the beginning and end of a novel as Hogan does. Or, it can signal a change coming in a relationship. It can be used to create a mystery or throw the reader off-guard a bit. And it can be used to introduce a hint of something to come (foreshadowing).

Consider ways you might work setup and payoff into your first fifteen pages. Or use setup in the first fifteen pages and payoff later in your book. Use the idea of setup and payoff to look through your pages and see if you've introduced something that you never intend to payoff. Readers hate when a writer introduces something, only to drop it from the story and never revisit it.

One of my favorite books from 2016 was *The Forgetting Time* by Sharon Guskin. If you haven't read it, I highly recommend it, with one suggestion, skip the first chapter. If you missed it, it is probably because the first fifteen pages should have been cut from the book. Guskin used the first fifteen pages to tell the reader that the protagonist of her story went on holiday, had an affair with a married man, got pregnant, and didn't even know the father's last name. She spent fifteen pages creating a relationship with a person who disappears from the story after the first chapter and describing an event that while resulting in the child at the center of the story wasn't the inciting incident. The inciting incident comes on page 27 where we learn something about Noah is different. Had the book started on page 24, I believe it would have had more impact. The first chapter felt like a setup. I kept waiting for the payoff, for dad to come back into the picture, for dad to be a cause of what was going on with Noah. I was halfway through the book when I realized the first chapter, the chapter that almost made me stop reading the book because it was stereotypical and the characters were unsympathetic, had nothing to do with the story except to explain that she'd conceived Noah from a one night stand. She could have accomplished that in one sentence and saved the reader the agony of a bad first chapter.

This is how books lose readers. Setting up a situation and not paying it off alienates your reader and leaves us waiting for something that is unimportant in the scheme of your story.

But wait, some of you are saying, you read that book even though the first fifteen pages weren't related to the inciting incident. Yes, I did. But did you? I picked up *The Forgetting Time* to see if I could use it as a comparative title for a book we were considering representing. If I hadn't been reading it for a specific purpose, chances are I might have put it down after the first chapter. I'm sure Guskin's agent, and editor championed the book because they liked the premise of the story enough to ignore an unnecessary first chapter. I wish they'd cut that first chapter and gotten to the inciting incident more quickly. If they had, I think more of you would know about this book. Check it out for yourselves and see what you think about those first fifteen pages. Are they necessary?

If you haven't already, this is a great time to ask yourself yet again, "Is my story starting in the right place?" If not, cut anything that is keeping us from getting right into the action of your story and keeping us from the true beginning.

Quirks and Eccentricities

In Chapter 3, we spent a good bit of time on character. I'd like to delve into the topic a bit more and discuss quirks and eccentricities in more detail. Adding quirks or eccentricities to a character is another layering technique you can use in later drafts of your book.

A quirk is a behavior or a mannerism that defines your character in some way. If your story has a character that is OCD you could show that character tapping his foot in a particular way before he begins walking. He could tap the toe of his foot three times on the pavement and then his heel before setting off. Or she could cap and uncap and recap a jar of pickles repeating the pattern for the number of pickles in the jar. The character trait is OCD. The quirk is how your particular character acts out the trait.

Let's look at another example. You have a character in your novel that works in a salon. He's required to wear the salon's signature black t-shirt with the logo on the front. But your character is a fashion maven and wouldn't be caught dead wearing a uniform, especially one as unflattering as a black t-shirt. So, he finds ways to make the uniform his own. He flairs out the bottom and the sleeves of one of his t-shirts. He hangs copper beads from the bottom of another. And on some days, he wears a sheer copper mesh poncho over his t-shirt. The stylist is eccentric. He isn't content to wear something conventional and is willing to go to great lengths to be different. These details show us a lot about who he is and what is important to him. If understanding his nonconformity is important to your story, find a way to show us.

Delicious details don't have to take a paragraph to describe. Consider the description of Dumbledore in *Harry Potter*. Rowling tells us his beard and hair were "both long enough to tuck into his belt." Can't you just see that? Dumbledore wasn't a corporate man like Mr. Dursley. Describing his hair and beard in this way signals that Dumbledore is eccentric.

The same techniques can be used for setting and timeframe. Rather than tell us that a character lives in a beautiful old house, in *The Keeper of Lost Things,* Ruth Hogan gives the house a name, Padua. And with that, Padua becomes a character in the story. It makes Anthony, the owner, a bit eccentric and a bit romantic. Who, after all, names a house? Naming the house is a delicious and unexpected detail that wasn't necessary, but made a big impact on the story for this reader.

Callbacks, Catalogs, and Word Choice

I want to take a minute to talk about investing in yourself as a writer. You've already done this by buying and reading this book. Continue to find ways to invest in your craft and never stop learning.

A few years ago, I attended Aspen Words a writing conference held each year in Aspen, Colorado. I was fortunate enough to work with David Lipsky. David has written articles for Rolling Stone and the New Yorker and books on West Point and David Foster Wallace. His book on Wallace, *Although of Course You End Up Becoming Yourself: A Road Trip with David Foster Wallace,* was made into a movie starring Jason Segel and Jesse Eisenberg. In David's class, I was reintroduced to writing techniques I'd long forgotten. I also saw how much you can learn from someone if you allow yourself to be open to the experience of learning. I wrote an essay based on that experience I share in the resources below. This section draws on some of the things I took away from working with David that will help you layer your writing. Thanks, David!

Callbacks
A callback is different from a setup. A callback is an object or a reference used to remind the reader that a concept or a thing is important either to the character or the story. In *The Firm*, Grisham refers to Mitch three times in the first fifteen pages as hungry. By doing

this, he is reinforcing that one of the reasons Mitch is willing to overlook the subtle warnings Grisham builds into the story that the firm and their offer is too good to be true is because Mitch is *hungry*.

In the essay "A Model World," Michael Chabon uses callbacks in humorous ways to remind us of small jokes used throughout the essay. At the beginning of the essay, Chabon's narrator refers to a new affair with a would-be actress named Jewel he's recently begun. Later in the essay, we learn that Jewel is actually Julia and she is married to someone who has the power to ruin a friend's career. The reference to the Jewel/Julia confusion reminds us about the affair.

Think about ways you can work callbacks into later drafts of your work either to remind the reader what is at stake or as humorous references to things that have occurred. Don't overuse callbacks. They are a technique for layering your writing, but not the only technique.

Catalogs
We all use catalogs whether we are aware of them or not. Catalogs are used to describe people, places, or things. We could tell the reader that a character is exceptionally tall, big as a house, and hairy. That list provides a basic description of the character, or we could write a descriptive catalog that draws an image of the character in the reader's mind. Consider this description of Hagrid in *The Sorcerer's Stone*. The underlined portion is the catalog:

> *He was almost twice as tall as any man and five times as wide. He looked simply too big to be allowed — <u>long tangles of bushy black hair and beard hid most of his face, he had hands the size of trash can lids and his feet in their leather boots were the size of baby dolphins.</u>*

Rowling begins with standard references to height and width, but then she provides a list of details that clearly define what Hagrid looks like.

A great catalog mixes two expected details with something completely different and unexpected. In the example above, the unexpected is the description of feet like baby dolphins. In "A Model World," Chabon describes a character as "irritable, paranoid, and unwashed." Irritable and paranoid are both personality traits, unwashed is a lifestyle choice.

Chabon could have said irritable, paranoid, and argumentative. But using unwashed causes us to start a bit, to see the character differently.

In *The Husband's Secret* Moriarty uses a catalog to share Cecilia's thoughts about her daughter's eating habits and reinforce how finding the envelope had exhausted her.

> *She should go in and confiscate the bag of chips, except <u>they'd all eaten salmon and broccoli for dinner without complaint, and she didn't have the strength for an argument.</u>*

Look at the lists and catalogs in your writing. Think about ways you can shake them up and use them to add a delicious twist to your writing.

Word Choice

Shakespeare once said, "a rose by any other name would smell as sweet." Perhaps, but a bunch of roses may not be the most effective description for the flowers your character brings to beg forgiveness. The words we choose signal a layer of care in our writing. Consider this sentence by Chabon:

> *He lay down on the hard grey carpet and allowed the* knuckles *of his spine to crack and relax.*

Using the word knuckles rather than merely spine gives a visual for the reader that is both unexpected and effective.

In *The Hunger Games*, the inciting incident of the story is the Reaping. The word reap invokes an image of the Grim Reaper, the specter of death. It also echoes the warning "You reap what you sow." There are a number of other words Collins could have used. She could have called it the Calling or the Choice, but Reaping has exactly the right eerie quality for a ceremony that leads to death for all but one.

Think about her use of the word tribute. Tribute is used ironically. To pay tribute is seen as an honor, it is a compliment, intended as praise. The tributes in *The Hunger Games* are lambs going to the slaughter, but the Capital holds them up as heroes for their districts. These were intentional choices the writer made to describe and explain the situation Katniss finds herself in.

Words matter. Make great choices.

Employing the Five Senses

Let's pretend you've written your first fifteen pages and now you are going back through editing and improving. That is a perfect time to begin layering your writing using the five senses: sight, sound, touch, taste, and smell.

In the passage where Handful describes her sack coat, she muses about "how many unwashed bodies had worn it before me, but they had all kindly left their scents on it." That line immediately conjures up a memory of clothing heavy with body odor.

In a passage a bit further on, Sarah provides a vivid description of her home using sound and smell.

> *"For a moment I stood just outside the room listening to the saber-fronds on the palmettos clatter around the house. The eaves of the piazza hissed. The porch swing groaned on its chains . . . [Mother's] maid Cindie had spent hours wetting and fastening Mother's wig with paper and curlers and the sour smell of it baking had nosed all the way up the stairs."*

Kidd goes a step further by using active verbs to personify the noises she describes. The eaves of the piazza "hissed." The porch swing "groaned." The smell of the wig was sour and the smell "nosed" all the way upstairs.

Layering using the senses and active verbs is more often than not the work of a third, fourth, or fifth draft. Few writers can infuse this level of detail and craft into a first draft. Great writers know that getting the ideas down in a first or second draft is only the beginning. Novels such as *The Invention of Wings* or *Hunger Games,* novels that become best sellers and movies, are the work of many drafts and attention to detail that comes through this type of layering.

Emotional Layering

One of the final layering techniques and perhaps the most difficult is adding emotion to your writing. Emotions are the signals and clues about how a situation is affecting a character or characters in your story. It isn't enough to tell us that a character is heartbroken, *show* us.

Before Hagrid gives Harry to Dumbledore:

> *He bent his great, shaggy head over Harry and gave him what must have been a very scratchy and whiskery kiss. Then suddenly, Hagrid let out a howl like a wounded dog.*
>
> *"Shhh!" hissed Professor McGonagall, "you'll wake the Muggles!"*
>
> *"S-s-sorry," sobbed Hagrid, taking out a large spotted handkerchief and burying his face in it. "But I c-c-can't stand it – Lily and James dead – an' poor little Harry off ter live with Muggles – "*

Rowling could have told us that Hagrid was sad or distraught. But instead, she tells us he howled like a wounded dog, which we all know is a haunting and deeply hurt sound. Then she shows him burying his face and stuttering through his grief. Rowling uses these layers, so we see and feel Hagrid's emotions.

After witnessing the beating of the slave in *The Invention of Wings*, Sarah describes the recovery of her voice in very emotional terms.

> *I remained mute for a week. My words seemed sucked into the cleft between my collar bones. I rescued them by degrees, by praying, bullying and wooing. I came to speak again, but with an odd and mercurial form of stammer . . . now there were ugly, halting gaps between my sentences, endless seconds when the words cowered against my lips and people averted their eyes.*

Reading this passage, you feel the struggle to speak, and the shame Sarah's muteness causes her. You feel her resolve and the embarrassment of those around her. You feel the emotion of wanting to say something but having the words trapped deep inside.

Evoking emotions allows us to empathize with your characters. They make us root for them, struggle with them, and cheer when they succeed. Without emotional layers, we may continue to read, but we will never fully invest in your story.

Your First 15

Consider all the layering techniques we discussed in this chapter. Go through and look for ways you can add delicious details to your manuscript. These details may come during the initial writing, but most writers add these layers in the third, fourth, and fifth drafts of their book.

Try to find places to infuse your writing with:

- Setups and payoffs
- Quirks and eccentricities
- Callbacks
- Catalogs
- Word choice
- Five senses
- Emotions

Chapter 10: The Value of an Outline

Writing without an outline is like doing a high-wire act

without a net.

—Joseph Finder

To Outline or Not to Outline – That is the Question

For some, the idea of knowing where your novel is heading before you start is blasphemy. And to those people, I would say, I bet I can tell a writer who worked from at least an outline from one who is what is referred to in Nano Writer circles as a "pantser." Pantsers write, as the term implies, by the seat of their pants, letting the plot and characters unfold as they go. Planners, on the other hand, embrace some form of planning ranging from a few major bullet points to a fully fleshed out outline.

Joseph Finder, author of fifteen thrillers, many of which have landed on bestseller lists, is a big advocate of outlining. Finder believes "writing without an outline is like doing a high-wire act without a net. Some people can do it, but wouldn't you really rather have a net? I would." On the advice of author friend Lee Child, Finder decided not to outline his book *Power Play*. The result was that *Power Play* ended up taking Finder "several months longer than usual, simply because I wasted a lot of time on plot and on characters that I ended up cutting out."

Even if you don't love the idea of creating a full-blown, turn-by-turn outline of your story, I highly recommend mapping out crucial elements for your first fifteen pages. Having a clear idea of the essentials – the who, what, where, when, and why of your story – is the best way to ensure that you've created a compelling first fifteen pages that will keep your readers engaged and asking for more.

Still not convinced? JK Rowling creates detailed charts for her books, plotting the major plot points and complications of the story. Rowling created the chart below for the book *The Order of the Phoenix*. If you look in the top left-hand corner of the page, you'll see the "why" of the book. Why were Harry and Dumbledore's Army able to thwart Delores Umbridge? Because *she didn't see it coming*. That is the note that guided Rowling throughout the book. At the beginning of the book, Umbridge seems to have the upper hand, but once the tables turn, every scene shows Harry and his friends staying one step ahead of Umbridge until she is carried away deep into the forbidden forest.

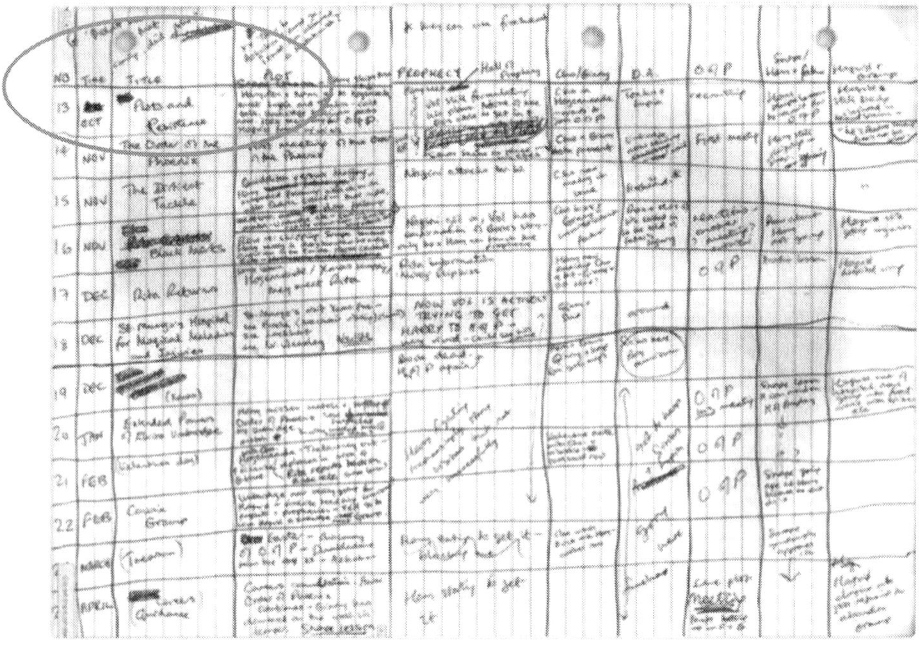

Figure 1. Chart used by JK Rowling to outline *The Order of the Phoenix*.

Rowling's chart is similar to the *Story Grid* spreadsheet developed by Shawn Coyne. I've used the *Story Grid* spreadsheet to outline my own books and to plan books with clients, and I've used it to analyze manuscripts we are considering taking on. It is a bit complicated and takes time to grasp, but I highly recommend taking a look at it if you plan to become a career writer.

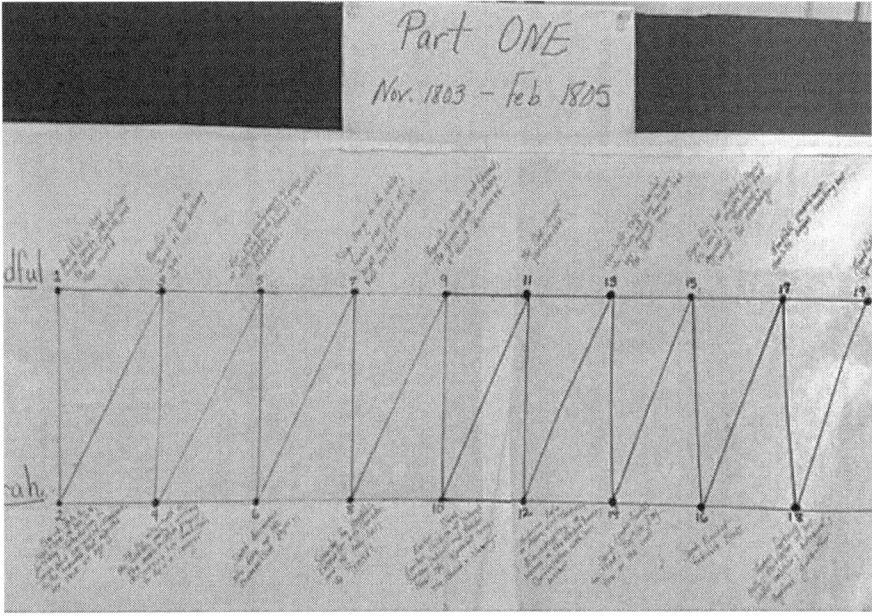

Figure 2. Chart used by Sue Monk Kid to outline *The Invention of Wings*.

Sue Monk Kid required a detailed outline for *The Invention of Wings*. When interviewed about her process she said that "due to the sweeping time frame and the voices moving back and forth, the outline for *The Invention of Wings* was the strangest one I've ever done." She broke the book down into separate outlines for each part of the book, writing them on "big butcher paper that was probably 2 feet long, and I used pencil because though I had a general idea of what would happen, I ended up changing it as I went." She hung the outline on the walls of her office so she could refer to it as she writes.

You can read more about Kidd's process in her interview on Oprah.com by going to the link on yourfirstfifteenpages.com under Resources.

Your First 15

Even if you don't end up outlining your story, you need an overall plan for your book. Before you begin writing, you should identify:

1. The why – the reason the story takes place. What will the reader learn or take away from your story? What inspired you to write it?

2. The inciting incident – the event that kicks off the story.

3. The characters that need to be introduced within the first fifteen pages to move the story forward. If they aren't necessary right up front, bring them in later when that character is needed to advance the story.

4. The timeframe(s), if it is vital to your story. Some stories jump between time frames – the Civil War and present day or the time of the Salem witch trials and present day. Define the period carefully and stick to it.

5. The setting – if the setting for your story is Oxford, England, and for some reason that setting has an impact on the story, this is something you need to include in your outline and show us in the first fifteen pages of your novel.

6. The point of view – who is telling the story? And are they relaying the story in first person or third? Do you have an omniscient narrator?

These are things you need to know before you begin writing. You can always write in first person and then write a scene again in third person until you get the point of view perfected for your story. Even if, after the first fifteen pages, you decide to switch the point of view to a different character, you need to give the reader a starting point and an anchor for the beginning of the story.

Resources

Download the *Your First Fifteen Pages* outline from Airtable.

Chapter 11: Most Asked Questions

"Writing the last page of the first draft is the most enjoyable moment in writing. It's one of the most enjoyable moments in life, period."

—Nicholas Sparks

How many drafts do I need before my manuscript is finished?

The short answer is as many as it takes. The long answer is until you reach a place where you know your manuscript is as good as you can make it and you are ready for others to breathe into your work and help it grow. An author, very rarely, creates a great novel entirely on their own. After the writer is finished with a manuscript and has worked through it with a writing group, editor, or at the very least, a trusted friend, it is sent off to an agent who, after reading it may make notes and suggestions, before sending the book out to editors. Once a book is signed, an editor or a team of editors, including a developmental editor and a copy editor, will make changes and suggestions to the manuscript before it is ready to go to print.

Here is another example from the class I had with David Lipsky. In 1996, Jonathan Franzen wrote an initial draft of his novel *The Corrections*. The opening line in 1996 was "The madness of an invading system of high pressure." The opening line of the book, after publication, is "The madness of an autumn prairie cold front coming through." The first draft tells us knowingly of time or place. The final version immediately sets us in place and time.

How many drafts? When you read through your novel, and there isn't anything else you can do to connect your reader to the who, what, where, when, and why of your story, it is time to share it.

What is the best way you know to learn to write?

In both my own writing and in teaching I use the technique I've used throughout this book – modeling. I believe we learn from watching. We learn by taking what someone else has done, and we try it for ourselves. After reading Michael Chabon's essay "A Model World," I decided to model it. I wrote a piece called "A Model Week." I used many of the techniques and the pacing I saw in Chabon's piece. I've included both in the Resources for this chapter so you can see how modeling works.

Take the beginning of a novel you love and see if you can use it as a model for your story. I'm not advocating plagiarism. There is no honor or art in ripping off someone's work, but using someone's structure, pacing, and style to create your own work has been done since the second person held a hammer and chisel to carve out the second story committed to stone. It is the seed of the inspiration we get when we read something and think, "I could write that so much better."

How long does it take to write a novel?

The short answer is you can write a novel in less than a year if you commit to writing 375 words a day. The word count range for novels runs from 80,000 to 120,000 depending on the genre. Let's take the high end. If you write 375 words every day for 365 days, you will have the first draft of a 120,000-word novel. Notice I said *first draft*. And you would need to write every day, but at the end of the year, you'd have a finished first draft. After that, it might take another year or two to polish, layer, and hone that draft into a manuscript you can begin sending out to agents.

The reality is, it is up to you. If you commit to writing every day. If you write more than 350 words a day. If you write for 2 or three hours a day and only take Sundays off to see your family, shower, and eat. You might be able to finish a draft in six months and have a polished manuscript in a year or a year and a half. But this depends on a lot of ifs. And it depends on what you are willing to give up. Are you willing to give up Facebook? TV? Time with the friends that you don't really like or get much out of being with? The other things that waste your time and energy? If the answer is yes, the chances are better you will get your book done and out to publishers sooner rather than later.

Who should read my book before I send it out to agents?

Anyone you can find who will give you honest and constructive feedback! Don't send a book to agents that you and you alone have read. We can tell if you are the only person who has ever laid eyes on your book. We immediately see the places where, if you'd had other eyes on your manuscript, the writing and the story would be stronger and basic mistakes would be fixed.

Find a tribe. Find writers who are willing to share their work and are willing to look at yours. Local libraries have writing groups. Meetup and Facebook are great places to look. Local bookstores know if there are writing groups in the area and often host writing groups. Ask friends if they know anyone who is a writer. If you live out in the boonies of Alaska, find a writing tribe online. I have two writing groups. My local group meets every Wednesday. My other tribe is spread coast to coast. We have members in eastern and western Canada, Washington, California, and Alabama. We meet a couple of times a year and virtually whenever one of us needs help.

The point is there are ways you can find writers, editors, and readers that will help you grow your work. Take advantage of the opportunity to learn from others and to help others write. Listen to what your tribe tells you about your work and be open to feedback. If you find that the advice they give you resonates, take it. If not, be grateful and move on. Your writing will grow, and your book will be better because of the collaboration!

How do I get an agent?

Write a great book. No, seriously? *Seriously*, write a book that tells a complete and compelling story. Use the techniques discussed here. Work with a tribe and then rewrite and rewrite and rewrite until you have a layered story full of delicious details, captivating characters, an intriguing inciting incident, and clear who, what, where, when and why, and you won't have a problem finding an agent.

That said, one of the hardest ways to get an agent is by cold querying. Many agents don't even read their slush pile. They only sign writers referred by other writers or editors or someone they know. Or, they court writers who've written for a magazine, journal, or blog.

That brings me to the first way to get an agent. Write. Send your work out to journals, magazines, and competitions. A number of writing competitions are juried by agents, so contests and competitions are a great way to get noticed.

Another way to find an agent is to attend writing workshops and conferences that include agents and editors. Don't be shy! Especially if you've paid to attend the conference. Have a great pitch (two to three sentences) ready for your book in case you find yourself sitting next to an agent. When asked what you are working on, pitch your book! If the agent tells you to send it, follow up!

Go to book festivals and support other writers. You never know who you might meet. I know writers who met their agents at book talks and festivals. I am presenting at a festival this month. And I'll be answering questions and talking to writers while I'm there. Go to where book people are, and agents will likely be in the mix.

And get to know authors. One writer I know became a huge fan of a new author. She went to her signings, said great things about her book on social media, and then when her book was ready, she mentioned she'd finished and was looking for an agent. The author asked to see her book. And after reading it, she passed it on to *her* agent who signed the writer fan. Support other writers and they will in turn support you.

Your First 15

For all writers:

1. Find a writing group in your area.

2. Pick one or two new authors and begin supporting them. Read their books, give them shout outs on social media. Love on them. Learn from them.

3. Explore writing workshops, conferences, and retreats you can attend to make connection with other writers and to grow your work.

Resources

1. www.storytreefarmretreats.com We host Your First Fifteen Pages workshops and retreats at Story Tree Farm.

2. https://www.pw.org/conferences_and_residencies Poets and Writers has a great database of conferences, retreats and residencies.

3. https://www.meetup.com There are writing meetups in cities and towns across America. Search for writing groups or writing and you're sure to find one close by.

Chapter 12: Tools

Today I introduce you to the most important tool in your arsenal: The humble kitchen timer.

Do you own one of these? If you don't own one, can you afford to go out and buy one? Do you maybe have a more modern interpretation of this device already on your smartphone?

Now here is what you do. At some point today, you sit down and set that timer for 30 minutes. Work on your craft or your project without interruption or distraction. Doesn't have to be major work — just has to be focused work. Don't get up from your seat until the timer dings. Then do the same thing tomorrow. And the next day. And the next day. And the next day…

—Elizabeth Gilbert

I've mentioned a couple of the tools I use throughout this book. In this chapter, I'll explain more about my go-to writing tools and how and why I use them.

Airtable

Airtable is the cooler, hipper version of Excel. It is more visually appealing, easier to use, and takes far less time to manage, set up, and navigate than other spreadsheets and databases I've used. It also stores all of its information in the cloud, allowing you to access your tables from your laptop, phone, or tablet.

I use Airtable to create timelines for books we are working on at RO Literary. To track my own writing projects. And we use it to track our queries and responses.

For writers, I recommend taking a look at the Airtable templates I've provided for this book. These include the action-tracking template I created for *The Firm* and the Airtable template for Your First Fifteen Pages. Once you start using Airtable to track your writing projects, I think you will be hooked.

Story Grid

Think of *Story Grid* as a tool to add to your writing toolbox. It can help you see what is and isn't working in your story. And, it helps you pinpoint places where the action in your story isn't progressing and analyze why. It is also full of useful information such as the obligatory scenes required for specific genres, and how to incorporate internal and external genres into your story.

Story Grid is complex and takes a lot of dedication to figure out. But I believe you will find it time well spent. If you use *Your First Fifteen Pages* to start your novel and then use *Story Grid* to drive the remainder of your story, you will take advantage of the two best storytelling tools around.

Grammarly

Nothing says amateur writer more than when we receive a query submission full of grammatical errors. Think of your submission to an agent as a job interview. You are interviewing for the job of author. When we sign authors, we are signing someone we want to work with for years to come. We want to nurture and grow your writing career, not just one book. We are looking for people who are professionals. If you send us a query riddled with errors, we may not even look at your submission because what you are telling us is, you are sloppy, unprofessional, and don't mind wasting our time. Would you hire that person?

You don't have to be a grammar whiz to be a writer, but you do have to use the tools that are readily available to ensure the writing you submit is free of errors. One of the best tools we've found is

Grammarly. I use it for everything from writing to Facebook posts. Running an email, a proposal, or even a social media post through Grammarly might take a bit more time, but I've saved myself from sending out communication containing countless small errors and even from making an occasional large oops! You can also install the app on your browser, and it will check for issues in all your writing on that browser in real time like emails, forum submissions, and social media posts.

And Grammarly is free, so you don't have any more excuses for sucking at grammar.

Word

My writing tool of choice is Word. I prefer Word for a couple of reasons. I grew up on it, so I know it inside and out. And most of the editors I know and work with use Word. It is the industry standard, which is the best reason for sticking with it. If you want to be a true professional, find out what the industry uses, learn it, and use it.

Given it is the industry standard, there is a good chance when you receive edits on your book from an agent or an editor they will use Word and most likely a feature called Track Changes. If you are completely unfamiliar with Word or Track Changes, the learning curve to edit your book will be steep. Getting to know these tools now, will save a lot of time and heartache later.

The drawback to Word is that it wasn't designed for writing a book. Although there are different views possible in Word such as outline and publishing view, these don't really give an overall view of a book or allow you to move scenes around without risking losing chunks of writing.

Scrivener

I know a number of writers who use Scrivener and love it. Scrivener was created specifically for books and screenplays. Your book is laid out according to chapters and scenes, which can easily be moved around because each is a distinct unit. You can view your book in Corkboard Mode, allowing you to grab virtual index cards and move them around if you decide to reorganize your book. It also has some nice project tracking features so you can see how many words you type a day and set goals to meet specific targets. I use Airtable for this, but if you use Scrivener, it's nice to have it built in.

The big con of Scrivener for me is the lack of a great editing tool. And the lackluster formatting functions. It is nearly impossible to produce a visually stimulating document straight out of Scrivener. Many writers I know write in Scrivener and then run it through Word to format and compile.

Freedom

Perhaps one of, if not the, most valuable tool I've found, is a little app called *Freedom*. Ironically named, Freedom virtually handcuffs me to Word and makes it impossible for me to open social media or Huffington Post while I'm writing. I invested in Freedom about six months ago, set up my writing schedules from 6:00 a.m. to 11:30 a.m. and from 1:30 p.m until 4:30 p.m., and watched my productivity shoot through the roof.

The only downside I've seen to Freedom is the rare occasion when I need to access the internet for research, I get the blank screen with the green Freedom butterfly and I can't get the information I need. I've learned to highlight the section in my document and move on. When my Freedom session ends, I go online, look up what I need, and remove the highlights.

I highly recommend Freedom or a similar tool if distractions are keeping you from starting or finishing your book.

Notebooks and Journals

My favorites are Moleskin and those by Rifle Paper, but I have journals in every size and from every place I visit. Always have a journal to write down an idea, a conversation you overhear that can become dialogue, a sketch of an outfit someone is wearing, a description of the ocean and the light on a particular day. Yes, I also use Notes on my phone and I transcribe my notes into Evernote a few times a year so I can index and tag ideas and find them. But for me, nothing replaces a good pen and a journal for capturing the world as it passes by.

Your First 15

Resources from this chapter:

Airtable

Freedom

Scrivener

Word

Story Grid

Chapter 13: Cultivating Passion

You start with infatuation, obsession, passion, anger, zeal, craze, then take a handful of notes, and sew them into a chord structure, create a melody over that, then come up with the words that fit it perfectly. Oh my god, what is that?

—Steven Tyler

Rock Legend, former American Idol Judge, and author of *Does the Noise in My Head Bother You?*

I am obsessed with the reprise of "American Idol." Not much on TV has held my interest for very long over the last five years. I can't imagine spending hours watching the fourth, fifth, or yowza the tenth season of anything. As a writer, investing that much time and energy into TV is the equivalent of the cramp I get in my foot right after I get into bed. It keeps me from doing what I want to be doing, which is sleeping. Watching endless hours of TV keeps me from what I want and should be doing, reading and writing. So why am I obsessed with "Idol?" Passion, commitment, and confidence.

Passion, commitment, and confidence go a long, long way in the publishing business. To be a successful author, it isn't enough to write a beautiful story. You have to *believe* in your work. You have to *sell* your book to agents, editors, and readers. No one will do that for you. And to sell your work, you need passion.

Let's get clear on the definition of passion for writers. Passion isn't about suffering. It isn't agony or anger. Passion, the good kind of passion, is about devotion to your craft, belief in what you are creating, being excited to share it with others, and the joyful pursuit of all the things that go along with being an author.

Watching "Idol," I can almost predict who will move forward and who will hear those dreaded words, "This is the end of the line." The contestants who bring their "A" game each week bring passion. They are dedicated. They are the people staying up the latest and getting up the earliest to practice. They go to bed thinking about music and wake up dreaming about how to make their performance even better. They believe in themselves from the bottom of their musically inclined toes to the tip-top of the highest note they can hit. *They know they are the next American Idol.* They are excited. Not just to be there, but to be there with the other contestants, coaches, and everyone who is putting time and energy into the experience. And they are in joyful pursuit of their goal. They aren't harping on what happened yesterday or even five minutes ago. They are embracing and learning from everything they do and building those lessons into who they are and will be as an artist.

I see the same thing when I look at queries or talk with writers at conferences or in classes. Writers who view writing as "hard," who find little joy in their work, who don't learn or grow after the first, second, or third draft or the first, second, or third book, those who don't embrace and appreciate the people pouring love and effort into their books, will never be as successful as those who work with joy, learn and grow.

Think about that for a minute. Think about the writers we've talked about in this book. What do you know about them, as writers, apart from the books you've read? JK Rowling spends hours on Twitter every week thanking her readers and encouraging writers and fans.

John Grisham's latest book is set in a bookstore. He recently did a book tour for *Camino Island* and strongly encourages best selling writers to go to bookstores. "We should go to bookstores, to say thanks to the booksellers, to meet fans, and sign autographs."

Sue Monk Kidd recently put a post up on Twitter about attending a book signing at her local bookstore with #fangirl.

Liane Moriarty is passionate about writing and authors. She strikes a nice balance between promoting her own books on Facebook and those of other writers.

Suzanne Collins has remained very private as an author, but when *The Hunger Games* came out, she actively promoted it on Facebook and in a very funny way on Twitter.

I know a number of published authors. I recently attended a book talk by one of my favorite writers and dear friend Robert Hicks. The talk was for a group of women from Mississippi who had read *The Widow of the South* and came to Franklin to tour Carnton Plantation, the setting for the novel. Robert met the group after going through a round of chemo that morning, and despite being a bit tired, he gave the women two hours of his time, answering every question they had. Robert could have said no. He could have begged off using chemo as his reason. Everyone would have understood. But he didn't want to disappoint the group, and he wanted to support Joel and Carol, the owners of Landmark Booksellers in Franklin, Tennessee. That is passion and commitment.

If you are writing historical fiction and haven't read *The Widow of the South* or *Orphan Mother* by Robert Hicks, these need to go at the top of your reading list.

Your First 15

Writing is only the beginning. To become an author you have to show up, find ways to tell the story of your book over and over and over again. Sell books, talk with readers, and support bookstores. You have to be passionate about this business. If you aren't sure how to do that, find authors to follow. Watch "American Idol," attend author talks and tell the author "thank you." Promote the books of authors you love without expecting anything in return. Practice gratitude.

Resources

1. *You are a Bad Ass* by Jen Sincero.

2. Your local bookstore events page.

3. American Idol

4. Facebook, Twitter, and Instagram, and websites for authors.

Chapter 14: Ready, Set, Query

I'm going to switch to agent mode for this chapter. See that picture? That's how it feels when I look at my inbox. While I'm incredibly grateful to be on this journey with you and would love to respond to every submission, the reality is that there aren't enough hours in the day to send out a thoughtful response to every query we receive.

When we first started our agency, Laura and I tried to respond personally to every single query we received. But as our inbox continued to fill, we got further and further behind on reading queries. So, we tried shortcutting the process by sending out a form email, hoping that hearing something from us, even if it was general, was better than feeling ignored and rejected. That approach seemed to help a bit. Writers emailed us back thanking us for "acknowledging my query, even if it was just a form email, at least I don't feel like my query fell into a black hole." But, every time we sent out the form, we cringed a little. We didn't feel like a form response to queries fulfilled one of the key missions we had when we started, which was to help writers grow their work and pass along as much information about the process as we possibly could.

We've pondered the query/response issue for months. As writers ourselves, we know how disappointing it can be to hear crickets when sending out a query. But as a small boutique agency, we struggle to find time to read and respond to every query we receive in a meaningful way. After much debate, we think we hit on a solution. It isn't perfect, but we believe it helps bridge the gap between no response and information that will help you move your book forward. The rest of this chapter unpacks what happens once we receive your query and sheds light on why we, and most agents, pass on a submission.

I've included the information we send out after receiving a query in the hope you find it helpful and illuminating. If you've sent out queries and find that your query falls into one of the categories listed below, don't panic! Knowing why something isn't working is half the battle. Go bac and revise your manuscript before sending your work out to other agents.

When We Receive Your Query

It is incredibly important that you submit your query *using the process each agent uses*. You can find submission guidelines on each agent's website. We use a form that sends all the queries we receive directly to a table on Airtable. The queries are logged in with a time/date stamp, so we always know when a query was received and which is next in line.

We try to read 5-10 queries a day. Reading a query can take a few minutes or as long as 30 and 45 minutes. Here is the process we use:

* We read your query letter in the order it was received.

* If we spot one of the reasons we generally pass with love, we move on. These include genres we don't represent and word count too high or too low for your genre.

- If we found your query compelling but are passing for a specific reason, and if we can't get you or your story out of our minds, we will send an email telling you why we passed and offer what advice we can to help you along your writing journey. This is rare, but it does happen.

- If we are intrigued by your query, we open the first fifteen pages of your manuscript or your book proposal (nonfiction only) *if* you follow the guidelines and attached your pages to your query.

- If you didn't attach the first fifteen pages or your book proposal, (even though we specifically ask you to in a number of places on our website) and we are still intrigued, we *might* send an email asking for the first fifteen pages or your proposal. Please don't make us do that!!! If we are intrigued but on the fence, chances are, we will move on to the next query. Again, think of this as a job interview. Would you want to work with someone who doesn't follow simple instructions? If we sign you, we will be working together. We want to know that you take this work seriously. Following the guidelines shows us that you do. Same is true for writers who email us directly and don't use the form. Those writers aren't following the guidelines. Rarely do we read those queries.

- If we LOVE the first fifteen pages or your proposal, we will send a request for more. We know how exciting receiving a request for a full manuscript is, but please keep in mind, it is still early in the process. Think of a request for a full as the second date, dinner after the first coffee date. We aren't engaged yet, but we are interested. Very few, very *very* **very** few, requests for additional pages turn into an offer of representation. VERY few. To take the next step, we have to love everything about your book — the story arc, the characters, the beginning, the middle, and the end. And we mean LOVE, as in we cannot live without representing this story. We cannot imagine our lives without the experience of having your book and you as an author in our lives for the next year or two or twenty. If we don't feel that way about your book, it would be a disservice to you for us to sign you. We've learned this lesson the hard way over the last few years, which is why we sign very few books. We are a small agency, which requires us to be extremely selective.

If you don't hear from us, we either haven't read your query or we've decided to pass. The queries we are interested in will result in an ask for more. Again, we are so so sorry we don't have time to send each person a personal response. We need to spend our time reading everyone's query. The same is true for many of the agencies you are querying. Try not to take a no or silence personally. There are valid reasons we've passed.

The Most Common Reasons Agents Pass

After reading thousands of queries, here are the most common reasons we don't move forward after reading your query:

- We do not represent your genre.

- The query is poorly written or dead boring.

- The premise doesn't grab us or hold our interest.

- The word count is too low or too high.

- The sample pages need more work, which means the manuscript isn't ready.

- Your social media numbers and web presence are low or non- existent (for non-fiction).

Let's look at each of these in detail.

You submitted a query for a genre we don't represent.
This is our easiest pass. We are very clear in our submission guidelines and on our About Us page about what we do and do not represent. If you submit science fiction, children's books, erotica, or any of the genres we don't rep, we immediately pass on your query. Reading the guidelines for every agent you query will help save time for you and the agent and ensure you aren't waiting for a reply from an agent that

wasn't a good fit for your manuscript because of genre. We really can't emphasize this enough. Querying is not a one size fits all proposition. Read the submission guidelines for each agent you query and follow the guidelines.

The query is poorly written or dead boring.
I can't say this enough, think of this as a job interview. You are applying for the job of writer. And yet, many writers dash off poorly written query letters, full of grammatical errors that read like an afterthought. You get one shot, two minutes at best to grab our attention and make us want to know more about your story and you as a writer. Your query letter needs to be engaging. It needs to get us excited about your story. It needs to pique our interest and compel us to ask for more. That is the sole purpose of a query letter. Sell us your story. Once a publisher signs your book, you have to switch from author to promoter and salesperson. Get in that mode when you write your query. Sell it! We offer a lot of advice on writing query letters on our blog and our podcasts at roliterary.com.

The premise doesn't grab us or hold our interest.
We are big readers. If we aren't reading queries, we're reading the Advanced Reader Copies (ARCs) we picked up at Book Expo or get from publishers, or the books we purchase ourselves from independent bookstores, or those recommended by friends or people we follow on social media (thank you Reese Witherspoon) or we are listening to books while we are driving, getting dressed, or doing chores (yes we have houses, with laundry, and families who need to eat just like you do). We are in this business because we are passionate about books and writers. But just like you, not every story jumps out at us. If a premise doesn't grab us, we aren't the agent for you. Don't take it personally. Keep querying. If the writing is there and the story is great, the right agent will come along.

The word count is too low or too high.
This one is fairly easy. The publishing industry has basic standards. We get frustrated when we see posts in writing groups where writers advise other writers to ignore the standards. These conversations begin with a new writer asking about word count, followed by a well-meaning writer advising that *their* opus is "250,000 words," so a book can be as long as

it needs to be." Or, "you are the writer, you know best how long your story should be."

CATEGORY	WORD COUNT
Short Story	Less than 5,000 words
Novelette	7,500 – 17,500
Novella	17,500 – 40,000
Novel	80,000 – 120,000 (depending on genre)
Memoir	75,000 – 110,000
Narrative non fiction	80,000 – 110,000
Self-Help	50,000 – 85,0000

The chart above shows the standard guidelines. The ranges are targets for you to consider. Most adult fiction and memoirs fall in the 80,000 to 100,000-word range. Historical fiction can be a bit longer. But that is the sweet spot for publishers and readers. If you submit a manuscript that is significantly under 80,000 words or significantly over 100,000, we will wonder if your book is underwritten or needs a serious edit.

When we send out an email stating that the word count is too low or too high, we often get a response back saying "Hey I know there are exceptions and my book is one of them!

Okay, let's look at that argument. When J. K. Rowling submitted Harry Potter, every major publisher in the UK turned down the book. One of their concerns was that the books were too long to hold the interest of young readers. So how was Rowling able to move past the word count hurdle? Her story was fascinating, her characters were complex, the setting was unique, and the books were incredibly well-written. Story and writing won out over word count. Those rare gems are exceedingly hard to find.

The sample pages need more work. The manuscript isn't ready.
This is one of the most heartbreaking passes for us. We read your query letter, and we were intrigued enough to open your first fifteen pages or your proposal, but after diving in, the manuscript felt like a second or third draft rather than a polished manuscript ready to go out to publishers. *Agents are not* book coaches, developmental editors, or copy editors. It is not our job to polish your manuscript. We do work with authors we sign to take their manuscript to the next level, but we only do that with manuscripts that are polished, free of typos and grammatical errors, and well developed. Our job is to sell your story to editors and get you a book contract. We cannot take an unpolished manuscript out to editors.

If you are the only person who has ever seen your manuscript, it isn't ready. Find a tribe of writers to share your work with. Find beta readers. Hire an editor. This doesn't have to cost a fortune. Local librarians, English teachers, and others enjoy editing and charge reasonable rates to edit books. Get your books in the hands of readers who will give you honest feedback and then consider their suggestions. Read your book out loud and record yourself. You'll be amazed at the hiccups you will find in your dialogue, pacing, and overall story when you read it out loud. Make another pass, then another. Then and only then, should you send your book out to agents.

While working on this book, I read a submission that begins with a young woman from a small town in Alabama dreaming of her wedding day. When the young woman wakes, she looks at her wedding dress hanging in her wardrobe. We see her caress the dress lovingly before she heads down to breakfast. Her internal dialogue and her actions create the image of a young woman anticipating her wedding day. As she moves through her day, we learn she is from a small town. We learn her mother is the town's midwife and that she has prophetic dreams. Her mother's actions cast an uncertain shadow over her daughter's joy over her upcoming nuptials. By the end of the first fifteen pages, we find the young woman's fiancée has jilted her and married another woman.

The main character in this story is intriguing, the setting is a small town where everyone knows everyone's business and is nicely depicted, the inciting incident is compelling. The string of actions leading up to the inciting incident piqued my curiosity. I wanted to know why the young man jilted her. They seemed to be, by her account, very much in love. Did he get someone pregnant? By the end of the first fifteen pages, I wanted to know more. Does she leave her small town? Does she become a bitter old maid? Does she inherit her mother's ability to see things? Can the author deliver on the promise of those first fifteen pages? I won't know unless I send a request for a full manuscript. What I do know is that out of the 133 submissions I've read in the last few days, this was the only one that provided a clear sense of time and place, interesting characters, an intriguing inciting incident, backed up with strong writing. Those are the types of queries and submissions we get excited about.

The social media and web presence are low or non-existent.
This applies primarily to nonfiction. If you've written a nonfiction book, agents and editors assume that you are an expert in your area. If you believe you are the next Chip and Joanna Gaines or Tim Ferris, editors will expect to see a social media following and a professional web presence. If you hope to enter an ongoing conversation, editors will want to know you have established yourself as a thought leader and influencer. Without a following, selling self-improvement, how-to, or a big-idea book to editors will be tough. Memoirs fall into this category as well. The unfortunate truth is that numbers drive nonfiction decisions these days. If you've been toiling away on a nonfiction book, spend some time building your platform before submitting to agents. And be sure that your book (or memoir) and your proposal is as well-written as it is helpful or telling.

Your First 15

We offer a lot of advice on querying on our blog and on our podcasts. You can find them here: http://www.roliterary.com/blog. And, you can find our podcast, The Literary Lunch on our website and iTunes.

Chapter 15: Final Thoughts

"I may not have gone where I intended to go, but I think I have ended up where I needed to be."

—Douglas Adams

I began this book with a quote from William Faulkner on reading. For writers, there is no better way to learn the craft of writing than to read. Read widely. Don't be a reading snob. Don't limit yourself to one genre. Read everything you can get your hands on. Read a book that resonates with you at least twice. Once for story and then a second or third or even fourth time for craft.

We recommend exemplars to every writer we work with. We do this because, as we've seen throughout this book, we learn from other writers. We learn about how to structure a story, create dialogue, develop characters, position a reader in space and time, and create the natural complications, dilemmas, decisions and indecisions that are part of life.

You've seen how we use these exemplars. Now it's time to strike out on your own. Explore other books in your genre. Take the books you love and map the first fifteen pages using what we've discussed here. Then use what you learn to write or rewrite your own novel or memoir.

Finishing a book is a massive accomplishment. Only twenty percent of those who say they want to write a book actually finish their book. The number is significantly smaller for those who go on to get their book published. I believe one of the obstacles between writing and publishing is making your submission so good agents and editors beg for more. That is why I wrote this book. I want to be able to make the big ask for more of the submissions we receive. I want to see *your* book on the shelves of a bookstore.

I hope *Your First Fifteen Pages* moves you closer that goal. I hope to hear someday that this book played a part in helping you move from idea to manuscript to a finished book and ultimately to published author. Nothing would make me happier! We will be adding more examples to the website – www.yourfirstfifteenpages.com. Please subscribe to receive updates, announcements, and additional tools.

Wishing you happy and productive writing,

Sandra

SAMPLE AIRTABLE WORKSHEETS

Sample Airtable Worksheets are available on the Your First Fifteen Pages website (yourfirstfifteenpages.com) under Resources. Follow the links to view the samples we've provided or to download the blank worksheet form you can use for your own stories.

YOUR NOTES

Printed in Great Britain
by Amazon

41443124R00088